The Paper-Hanger's Companion: A Treatise On Paper-Hanging: In Which the Practical Operations of the Trade Are Systematically Laid Down: With Copius Directions Preparatory to Papering; Preventions Against the Effect of Damp On Walls; the Various Cements an

James Arrowsmith

THE

PAPER-HANGER'S COMPANION:

A TREATISE ON

PAPER-HANGING;

IN WHICH THE

PRACTICAL OPERATIONS OF THE TRADE ARE SYSTEMATICALLY LAID DOWN:

WITH

COPIOUS DIRECTIONS PREPARATORY TO PAPERING;

PREVENTIONS AGAINST THE EFFECT OF DAMP ON WALLS;

THE VARIOUS CEMENTS AND PASTES ADAPTED TO THE SEVERAL
PURPOSES OF THE TRADE;

OBSERVATIONS AND DIRECTIONS FOR THE PANELLING
AND ORNAMENTING OF ROOMS, &c

BY

JAMES ARROWSMITH,

AUTHOR OF "AN ANALYSIS OF DRAPERY," ETC.

PHILADELPHIA:

HENRY CAREY BAIRD,

INDUSTRIAL PUBLISHER,

No. 406 WALNUT STREET.

1874.

PREFACE.

If the practical experience, with suitable attention to his business, during a term of fifty years, can entitle a workman to hope for some attention from his brethren in the trade, little apology will be requisite for offering the results of his various practice, with some degree of confidence that his efforts may be of that utility which he reasonably anticipates.

Since the reduction on paper-hangings, the putting up of them in too many cases has been intrusted to persons of various callings, and entire strangers to the business; and from the prevalence of this custom, it may fairly be inferred that the public generally are of opinion that the operation consists of the mere sticking the paper on the wall. It is needless to say much on the erroneousness of such ideas; the professed paper-hanger is aware of many difficulties which present themselves from various causes, and which have to be surmounted before the walls or grounds are in a state to receive the paper;* this is frequently too little attended to.

Modern economists deceive themselves in the belief, that as Dick, Jack, or Tom will work at low wages by the day, that system

---

* During the long term of my business, I have paid every attention to means for obviating these difficulties; for each I have given directions which I found suitable to remove each of them, and in cases where I have succeeded, from my practice, or information from others, the statement will be found under the head of "Preparatory treatment of walls or grounds for papering."

is a cheap one; but on a little reflection they would be convinced of its incorrectness from the slow progress of the operation, and what they considered economical is quite the reverse: a *Paper-hanger* would do the work in half the time by the piece, and with less waste and cost than the slap-bang innovator.

In the following treatise, I have endeavoured to explain clearly the requisites for each department of work from the foundation. Some persons may think it unnecessary to commence with such an early part of the business; but I remember the time when such instruction would have been gratifying to me; from which I judge it may be acceptable to others in a like situation.

The few observations on colouring in distemper, and hanging walls with cotton, may, I trust, be considered worthy of notice.

1*

In conclusion, I beg to draw attention to that part of the book relating to the care required in the management of hanging the crimson *stained ground* papers. I am not aware that my method has been practised, except by those I have informed of it; but if carefully attended to, I have no doubt of its proving useful, and preventing that disappointment and loss which I have witnessed, solely from mismanagement.

CONTENTS.

THE
PAPER-HANGER'S COMPANION.

Tools for Paper-Hanging.

THE tools required are few and well known; but as some of them may have to be occasionally referred to, I insert them here:—Pocket in front of apron, scissors, hammer, rule, plumb and line, sponge, straight-edge, paste-board, paste-pail and brush, size-kettle, and steps.

Before the commencement of the work, the following articles should be at hand, viz.: Pumice-stone, a basin of *clean* cold water, and a *clean* sponge, a wash-basin of water, and two or three soft towels. Where an apprentice or assistant is present, it is in his department to have them all ready.

I have to offer a few remarks on the paste-brush. I prefer the *large round* one; the would-be paper-hangers use the flat two or three knotted distemper brushes, under the supposition that they add to expedition; a professed workman knows better; they cannot take up the paste so clean and readily, neither can they be turned by the hand, as is required, to prevent daubing the stained side of the paper. I recommend to beginners to accustom themselves to the round brush; those who have used the distemper brush for a length of time, I have no doubt, will persevere in the use of it.

Pastes for Paper-Hanging.

I T is well known that it is impossible to make good adhesive paste of any other than flour from perfectly *sound wheat:* in critical and dear seasons various substitutes have been tried, but I never heard of sufficient success to induce a continuance of their use; and any flour from wheat which is the least unsound will only make a paste ready for the hog-tub; if allowed to stand a few hours, its adhesiveness is gone.

More depends upon the proper adaptation of the kinds of paste for the several purposes to which they have to be applied, than is taken into consideration. I believe, many of those persons who *attempt* paper-hanging use one kind of paste for all purposes, without regard to circumstances; but, as I am of opinion much depends upon the application of paste suitable to its purpose, I shall

enumerate those I have found best to answer my expectation in cases where 1 have
applied them.

No. 1.—*A Paste for General Purposes, prepared as follows:*—For a room which will
require about eight or nine pieces of paper,
beat up four pounds of flour with cold
water, but no more water at first than is
sufficient to make a *stiff* batter; beat it a
little, and small knots will not be formed;
then add more cold water to bring it to the
consistence of pudding batter as used in
cooking; add from one to two ounces of
well-pounded alum. (The above quantity
of flour will, when mixed, make paste to
fill three-quarters of a common-sized pail.)
Be sure to have more boiling water ready
than that measure; take it *quite* boiling
speedily from the fire, and pour it gently
and rather quickly over the batter, stirring
it at the same time; and when it is observed to swell, and the white colour of

the batter is changed, no more water is required. By attending to these instructions, a fine smooth paste will be produced.

When time permits, allow the paste to stand till cold before using it; if the paste is stiff while hot, you may put a little water, either hot or cold, just to cover the top to prevent its skinning; or you may leave it uncovered, but it should not be stirred up. Before using, take off every particle of skin, or straining may be required, which is troublesome. In using this paste for ordinary purposes, it may be thinned with cold water so as to spread easily and quickly with the brush. In cold weather it will keep a long time before it ferments, which reduces its adhesiveness; mouldiness at the top does not; take it off, and the remainder is good.

No. 2.—This paste must be made exactly in the same way as No. 1, with the exception *that no particle* of alum must come

into the composition, for the reason hereinafter explained.—*See pages* 37, 38 *and* 63, 64.

No. 3.—This paste is seldom wanted in
large quantities, and only where great adhesiveness is required; various methods are
used to make it so: I have found the following to answer my purpose:—In a brass or iron
pan, of a size according to the quantity of
paste required, mix flour with cold water in
the same manner as No. 1, but the batter
of much less consistence, and to two quarts
of this, add half an ounce each of pounded
alum and loaf sugar, and one ounce of resin;
this last must be very finely pounded, as it
does not dissolve so readily as the others:
set the pan containing the ingredients over
a moderate fire, constantly stirring it till it
boils and thickens, and a short time afterward; then put the paste to stand till cold
into a vessel calculated to leave the smallest
surface for the paste to skin over and to
prevent unnecessary waste, as the skin

must be entirely removed : then, as some adhesive liquid may be required to reduce its consistence, for the finest purposes, I recommend thin gum-arabic water as the best, and least of colour; or for coarser purposes, glue dissolved in ale or water over the fire, and of a consistence that, when cold, it may be sufficiently fluid to mix with the paste.

No. 4.—This paste must be made exactly in the same way as the foregoing No. 3, with the exception that no *particle of alum* must come into the composition, for the same reason as given for No. 2.

Sizing for Walls, &c.

I HAVE little to observe in the preparation of size. In large towns, it is to be procured either "double" or "single." I prefer that made from buffalo spetches, which is easy of preparation ; and, if made strong, will keep a long time, and can be readily reduced, when required, to suit every purpose. This size is harder, and not so soon in a state of decomposition as that made from the glue of commerce, which cannot be preserved long without becoming offensive.

Preparation of Walls or Grounds for Paper-Hanging.

It is highly essential to the attainment of neatness and perfection in paper-hanging, that the walls or grounds should be in a proper state to receive it. There are few things either in the arts or sciences which do not require a sound and clear foundation, and the preparation for paper-hanging is no exception to that rule. In domestic affairs I have heard an observation on cleaning an apartment, which, although trite, is true, and deserves due attention: "Clean out the sides and corners, and the middle will take care of itself." This adage holds equally good with my present subject, as experience has proved, and

2*

which I earnestly recommend to be followed by others.   Frequent cases occur in
practice which prove its necessity, and in
none more than in the next succeeding
article.

White or Coloured Walls in Distemper.

SINCE the reduction in the price of paper-hangings, many apartments are required to be papered, which had, for years previously, been whitewashed or coloured so frequently, that one coat upon another amounted to the thickness of a thin coat of plaster, and often fell off in flakes; all this must be removed by damping and scraping. A spatula for effecting this may be made of a worn plane-iron fixed into a piece of wood about half a yard long. At the flat end make a saw cut to receive the iron, and bind it firmly round the shaft, to be convenient to the hand, and it forms a ready implement. Care must be used to indent the walls as little as possible, as the blemishes will not be hidden by the paper Observe particularly, that the shell round

the top, bottom, and angles of the apartment, is taken off to the plaster; and the
same round the windows, doors, and fireplace. After puttying up with plaster of
Paris-putty, wash over the walls with hot
weak size.

I may observe, that, for common apartments *to be papered*, any inequalities may
be levelled up with a putty of whiting and
size; but for others plaster of Paris and
water is decidedly the best for stopping or
repairing walls preparatory to papering
them, but especially for walls or ceilings
which have to be finished in distemper, as
it does not contract on drying, as is the
case with that made of whiting and size.

To prove the great utility of plaster of
Paris in connection with paper-hanging, I
give the particulars in two instances, as examples to show how much it may be relied
upon.

Being employed to hang paper in a large
drawing-room, which had to be completed

on the second day after the commencement, a surbase had been taken down, leaving large plug-holes to be filled up. I proceeded as follows :—

Being provided with a small trowel, some pieces of bricks, a small dish, (such as is used for the table,) a paste-brush, water, and fine sifted plaster of Paris, (which is usually to be had in a suitable state from the plasterer.) First, with the brush I wet the aperture, then mixed as much of the plaster with cold water as with the pieces of bricks might nearly fill the opening; the plaster being of the consistence of very thin batter, when in this hot state it soon sets hard, and must be applied readily. Having filled the aperture to about a quarter of an inch beyond the surface of the wall, I then mixed a small quantity for facing up, of a similar consistence, and before I found it setting hard I added a little more water, working it with the trowel till the heat had sufficiently gone off to allow it to work like plaster; with this I made a smooth surface, which would have answered had it been for colouring in distemper.

I never could induce bricklayers to forbear using a small portion of lime-plaster mixed with it, which delays the work; there is no occasion for lime, except to save a little trouble. To prevent disappointment in pursuing the method I have named, I have always performed the work myself.

I should have been glad to avoid so much egotism, but I find by doing so I could not make myself so clearly understood, and therefore beg the reader's indulgence for it and this digression.

To resume the subject.—When I had got the walls prepared, I hung them with lining paper, and the next day finished with a delicate white satin ground paper, which when dry, had not the least mark or stain upon it to denote the parts repaired with the plaster of Paris.

I shall mention another instance, which may suffice. A bell-hanger, having to break through a wall of considerable thickness, was obliged to make an aperture (for placing the bell-handle) about eighteen inches in diameter : this was in the drawing-room of a mansion, and time not admitting of delay, the services of the bricklayer were in requisition; but as he would not undertake to close the opening without some addition of lime to the plaster of Paris, I engaged the carpenter to put up a facing of thick dry deal, placed nearly half an inch from the surface of the wall. The front of the deal was incised with a chisel, to form a key for the plaster; and to secure the deal in its place, I put up, previously to its being fixed, some bricks laid in plaster. The first coat of plaster I put on in its hot state, leaving the surface rough to form a key to the next cool coat, which was smooth and flush with the face of the wall. I immediately hung the walls with lining paper, and

the next day proceeded with a white and
gold paper, without the least mark or unevenness being visible on the part repaired
at that time, or at present, after a lapse of
sixteen years.

The two foregoing examples may be relied upon as being correct; and I hope may
be gratifying to those who have to resort
to means under similar circumstances, and
from their success be induced to excuse so
lengthened an article.

On the Preparation of Grounds affected with Damp.

DAMP is one of the worst adversaries the paper-hanger has to contend with, and various are the means resorted to for overcoming this formidable enemy. I shall mention those I have used myself, under the several circumstances which presented themselves, and have below endeavoured to class them in the order that I have found answered the best; following them, each consecutively, with remarks, and the methods I adopted to meet the difficulties.

No. 1. Battening for Lath and Plaster.

　2. Battening and Canvassing.

　3. Hameline's Patent Mastic.

　4. Sheet Lead.

5. Pitched Paper.

6. Strong Brown Paper.

7. Mixture of Clay with Paint.

8. Dry Rot.

9. Ivy on Exterior Walls.

It may be supposed that, with such a variety of expedients to overcome the difficulties arising from damp, some few of them might *infallibly* answer the purpose. My opinion is, that No. 1, only can be relied upon; but being attended with much trouble and expense, comparatively with other means, it is seldom resorted to, except when a new building is erecting, where persons of sense and spirit, who study their own comforts and interests, adopt it. In old apartments it is considered an insuperable difficulty to effect this operation; but a practical paper-hanger can always, by instructions to the proper workmen, remove it; he will recommend the plinth of the room to be taken off, and the walls plugged with oblong *square* plugs of some hard wood, which can be easily performed by the carpenter, according to the directions of the plasterer, who knows where the battens are to be placed, to suit the laths he has to use. Should it be objected that the battens project before the plaster cornice, still, should it be so, a little ingenuity will only be required to keep it from observation; but in general cases, the lower member or square of the cornice is sufficient to admit the thickness of the batten required, and where there is no plaster cornice there can be no obstacle.

No. 2. BATTENING AND CANVASSING.

I RECOMMEND this, but subject to the remarks in the succeeding No. 3, as the next best method. The experienced paper-hanger is the person to overlook and direct the carpenter, and he should always be consulted; carpenters are not generally acquainted with the power of contraction of paper as it becomes dry. Such persons imagine a few *pointed* plugs, put in here and there, are sufficient, and instead of battens, put up slating laths, or something of the kind in such arrangement as is unsuitable for the canvassing. I have, but unwillingly, finished papering upon such work, and seen it, when dry, turn out both the plugs and laths: this is no exaggeration, but literally true. Some employers are so stingy and obstinate from ignorance, that workmen like myself in such like case are obliged to submit, although aware of the mortifying result. Having now stated what should be avoided, I have endeavoured to explain in the following part of this article the method I recommend.

I have observed in No. 1, that plugs should be made of some hard wood in oblong squares, and of course in length and thickness commensurate to the purpose for which they are required. I object generally to tapered plugs, but they are too often used, it being less trouble to make the apertures to receive them than for those I recommend.

The kind of battens I have used for apartments about to be canvassed were three inches in width, and five-eighths of an inch in thickness: deal-wood is the most proper for the purpose.

The battens must be placed close to the top, bottom, doors, windows, and fireplace, and double to form a right angle at each of the corners, unless the shape of the apartment requires a deviation.

3*

All these ought to have plugs near their extremities; intermediate battens, about two feet apart, are required to support the canvas against pressure; but as there ought to be no *nailing* or stress against them, slighter plugging may suffice.*

To prepare for canvassing, observe, that as there must be no nailing upon the *intermediate* battens, the canvas must be cut and joined by back-stitching in sizes, that each may be sufficient to cover a side, an end, or such part as has to be papered: before putting up the canvas, heat it before a fire, it will stretch better, and use *tinned* tacks, as they do not rust. I prefer commencing with nailing at the top in the *centre* of any of the compartments, and drawing the canvas each way; by this means the threads

---

* In some cases, taking off the plinths of the apartment may be objectionable; then the plaster must be cut away to receive the battens, only leaving a small projection before the face of the wall, to prevent the canvas coming in contact with it.

of it are kept warp and woof at right angles, a matter of more consequence towards proper stretching than is generally attended to. When the top of the canvas is nailed, commence drawing it down also exactly in the centre as at the top, and from it strain it each way to the ends. By doing so firmly the work will be much tighter; the sides may be done in like · manner from the centre. When the battens are of the breadth I have given, there is no occasion to nail upon the selvages of the canvas, which form ridges; *cut them off*, and every way nail, so that an inch beyond the tacks may be pasted down; the tacks should not be more than three inches apart; and if this method is adopted, there will be no occasion for turning in of the canvas, if the pasting of it is suffered to dry before the hanging of the paper.

The kind of canvas I have found the best for the purpose, is that known as strainering canvas, used by upholsterers as their first stuffing canvas, and with as little sizing as possible in its manufacture.

I have been particular in giving these directions, having observed persons that should from experience have known better, under a false notion of expediting the work, use an incautious method leading to a disappointing result.

Stiff paste is required for canvassed grounds: that which is scalded as No. 1, will answer if properly made and suffered to skin over till cold; after taking off the skin, no more water should be added, and a round quantity put upon the paper: if the paste is too thin, the canvas will require pasting, which should be avoided.

N. B.—If the finishing paper is of the crimson *stained* ground kind, No. 2 *must* be used entirely from the first pasting of the canvas to the completion.

No. 3. HAMELIN'S PATENT MASTIC.

THIS ought, perhaps, from its general utility, to have been classed before No. 2; but in the present instance, for damp walls, I may be allowed to remark, that although it is readily procurable in London, with workmen conversant in its use, it is not so in the country, which is a matter of regret, considering the excellence of the mastic for the several purposes to which it is applicable: workmen in the country who might frequently make use of it to the advantage of their employers, so far as I know, never recommend it; they do not, or will not be at the trouble to acquire, although simple, the proper method of using it, yet attainable by a little practice.

Some years ago, in accordance with my constant desire to overcome the difficulties which damp walls opposed to paper-hanging or colouring them, I visited the establishment of the patentees, Messrs. Francis and White, Nine Elms, Vauxhall; from their politeness, on explaining to them my object, they obligingly set a boy (apparently about fifteen years of age) to show me the method of putting the mastic on a wall: this he did with as much care and expedition as any experienced plasterer could have performed his work to the same extent with plaster of lime. The coating which the boy put on was about three-eighths of an inch in thickness, with a perfectly even surface, which convinced me of its efficacy for my purpose. I can, therefore, with much confidence assert, that those who think proper to try the mastic as a remedy for damp walls, for papering, &c., will not be disappointed.

It is unnecessary for me to expatiate further on the suitableness of this for many other purposes, as it is frequently advertised in the newspapers by the patentees, and doubtless they will give every explanation to those who may make application.

No. 4. SHEET LEAD, AS MANUFACTURED IN ROLLS, AT THE LEAD MILLS.

I CANNOT recommend this more than a partial use of it: my experience has convinced me it is not deserving of more, except by a modification hereinafter explained; yet it is entitled to some regard in certain cases, which I shall point out in the proper place. The reasons of my objections are, that it is expensive, heavy, and, from its weight, difficult to be retained upon the wall when subjected to the contraction of paper-hangings while drying. I beg to be understood, this is my opinion in cases where the *entire walls* or *entire side* of an apartment requires a remedy, especially if the operation is performed in the usual way, that is, affixing it to the wall by nailing it in every part to the *plaster only;* and this is the chief reason why so much disappointment occurs in its use. To prevent a failure from this cause, I recommend in these cases I have mentioned, that the plaster around the top, sides, and both sides of the angles be cut away to receive battens three inches broad, and let in flush with the face of the wall, the battens being secured by plugs; without this precaution, the weight of the lead, and contraction of the paper as it dries, will, as I have seen, draw the nails from the plaster. The remaining part of the process may be the same as usually adopted, viz., where the lead is in one piece from top to bottom, overlay one breadth over the other, and nail with COPPER nails; where more than one piece is required to complete the length, the longer piece or pieces must overlie the one above it. The lead should be half an inch from the extremities, and the nails about three-quarters of an inch from the edges of the lead.

The inquiry may be made, Why is the batten omitted at the bottom? I answer, there is no stress from the weight of the lead, and should the damp not be extreme, by bringing the lead to within half an inch of the plinth, the trouble and expense may be saved; but this must depend upon circumstances and the judgment of the paperhanger.

Where more patches of damp appear on the walls, and distant from the extremities, in such cases lead is effectual; use copper or tinned tacks; the part being surrounded on every side by the paper-hangings, the lead will be secure. For such partial purposes, the lead taken from tea-chests, if whole, answers sufficiently.

The paste No. 1, when reduced to a moderate consistence, is sufficient, and it is well to put no more on the paper than allows it to adhere to the lead, as much strong paste adds to the weight, and causes more contraction in drying. When *stained* crimson-ground paper has to follow, use No. 2 paste throughout the process; for if

4

paste in which there is alum or any other acid, was used, it would affect the colour of the stained ground of the paper.—*See pages* 14 *and* 15.

No. 5. PITCHED PAPER.

THIS paper, prepared for sale by some of the paper-stainers, I have used, but cannot recommend it for any apartment where a fire is required; the smell is offensive when within the influence of heat : in vestibules, or places where there is no fire, it may answer the purpose of preventing the appearance of damp on a finishing paper; but in the first-mentioned case, it has been objected to by those who have submitted to its application. The following is, I believe, of equal efficacy, and unobjectionable as to the effluvia.

No. 6. STRONG BROWN PAPER.

A STRONG brown paper of immense size is now manufactured and used by warehouse-men, as a substitute for linen wrappers in packing goods of considerable bulk : this is occasionally a useful article to the paper-hanger, from its size and substance, and being made from materials in which some portion of tar enters its composition, renders it in a degree impervious to damp; as packages such as are mentioned are usually received by drapers and others in the country, the paper is generally procurable from them by those who are distant from the place of its manufacture.

When required for use, cut off the rough edges, and wet it well with water; let it lie till it is soft and pliable, as it is mostly in demand for partial purposes, such as putting over partial damp, or to level the unevenness of walls : it should invariably be put on with tinned tacks, and if it has to be entirely surrounded with the finishing paper, it will be sufficient and better to nail it only near the edges; in other cases, it must be left to the judgment of the paper-hanger how to proceed. I can only observe that I avoided passing it *whole* round the angles, and also avoided putting it quite close to the extremities of the parts to be papered, leaving sufficient space for the second or finishing paper to come upon the wall.

Nailing is more effectual than pasting, as it is evident, that if brought into close contact with the wall, the intention is partly, if not entirely, frustrated. I have used this paper and method successfully, and proved its usefulness, by the non-appearance of damp in affected places, which had been covered for some years.

No. 7. COMPOSITION OF CLAY AND DRYING PAINT.

I THINK it proper to be cautious in recommending this as an infallible remedy for damp walls requiring to be prepared or coloured, as I have not had experience, by practice, of its effect; yet I have much confidence in the composition answering the purpose, at least to the extent which good authority warrants me to state, and after doing so, I leave the matter to the judgment of those who require the aid of this or any other remedy.

A friend of mine, a painter of long experience and observation, was induced, from the circumstance of iron being present in a greater or less degree in most kinds of clay, to try the experiment of compounding it with drying paint as a repellent of damp, in which he was successful upon a portion of an interior wall which had baffled several previous attempts to subdue the damp sufficiently to prevent its appearance upon the subsequent colouring.

To prepare the composition, he dried some pure strong clay, (without regard to its analysis,) so that it could be pulverized and finely sifted, and then ground and mixed upon the stone, with litharge and strong-bodied paints, in oil.

This preparation was first tried by my informant upon a portion of a wall in a staircase. This occurred a few years ago, and recently I chanced to be present with my friend; when the gentleman in whose mansion the method had been tried called upon him in the way of business; and to the inquiry how had it answered? he replied, that he had seen no re-appearance of the damp since the means mentioned had been used. Subsequently, I have been informed that clay, such as bricks and tiles are made of, is the best for the purpose.

No. 8. DRY-ROT.

ALTHOUGH dry-rot does not occur so frequently as the preceding causes, to interrupt the operation of paper-hanging, yet, in my practice, I have several times met with its ramifications on interior walls, at a considerable height from the floor of the apartment. I shall relate a singular instance. Some years ago, I was engaged in the way of my business by a gentleman, to examine the cause of a large round black appearance upon the silk damask hanging on the wall in his drawing-room. On laying the wall bare, by removing the damask, I found a completely formed fungus, the size of the crown of a hat, and compressed by the damask to nearly an inch in thickness. This he retained as a curiosity.

In this case, through the recommendation of an experienced chemist, I applied a wash of aquafortis to the affected parts; which I believe was effectual; but I consider the following extracts on the subject worthy of attention : they are from the published work of a gentleman highly celebrated and esteemed for his indefatigable researches in every department of Natural History.*

"Dry-rot is a misnomer. This disease on timber ought to be designated a decomposition of wood by its internal juices, which have become vitiated for want of free circulation of air.

"If you rear a piece of timber, newly cut down, in an upright position in the open air, it will last for ages. Put another piece of the same tree into a ship, or into a house, where there is no access to the fresh air, and ere long it will be decomposed.

"But should you have painted the piece of wood which you placed in an upright position, it will not last long; because, the

---

* Charles Waterton, Esq. Longman, Orme & Co. London, 1838, p. 284.

paint having stopped up the pores, the in-carcerated juices have become vitiated, and have caused the wood to rot. Nine times in ten, wood is painted too soon. The up-right unpainted posts in the houses of our ancestors, though exposed to the heats of summer and the blasts of winter, have lasted for centuries; because the pores of the wood were not closed by any external application of tar or paint; and thus the juices had an opportunity of drying up gradually.

"In 1827, on making some alterations in a passage, I put down and painted a new plinth, made of the best, and apparently well-seasoned foreign deal. The stone wall was faced with wood and laths; and the plaster was so well worked in the plinth, that it might be said to have been air-tight. In about four months, a yellow fungus was perceived to ooze out between the bottom of the plinth and the flags; and on taking up the plinth, both it and the laths, and the upright pieces of wood to which the laths had been nailed, were found in as complete state of decomposition as though they had been buried in a hot-bed. Part of these materials exhibited the appearance of what is usually called dry-rot; and part was still moist, with fungus on it, sending forth a very disagreeable odour. A new plinth was immediately put down; and holes 1½ inch in diameter, at every yard, were bored through it. This admitted a free circulation of air, and to this day (eleven years since this took place) the wood is as sound and good as the day on which it was first put down.

"The same year, I reared up, in the end of a neglected and notoriously damp barn, a lot of newly-felled larch poles; and I placed another lot of larch poles against the wall, on the outside of the same barn: these are now good and well-seasoned: those within became tainted the first year with what is called dry-rot, and were used for firewood.

"If, then, you admit a free circulation of air to the timber which is to be used in a house, (no difficult matter) and abstain from painting that timber till it be perfectly seasoned, you will never suffer from what is called dry-rot.

"The long arrows which the Indians use in Guiana are very subject to be eaten by the worm; in 1812, (twenty-six years ago,) I applied the solution of corrosive sublimate to a large quantity of these arrows; at this hour they are perfectly sound, and show no appearance that the worm has ever tried to feed upon them."

No. 9. IVY ON EXTERIOR WALLS.

THE last thing I have to mention on the subject of damp relates to ivy on exterior walls of buildings, which may be said to belong more to the consideration of the architect than to my purpose; but as precaution is allowed to be better than cure, I trust it will not be thought irrelevant to notice its effect on internal walls, which is, that if it does not entirely eradicate damp, it may be admitted to be a repellent placed on the exterior.

I had my attention drawn to a case of this description, where damp had prevailed for a length of time in the walls of an apartment, but ivy having grown up to cover the opposite exterior side, the affected parts inside had become dry.

The gentleman in whose house I observed the improved change, accounted for it, I think with much reason, viz :—that the close overhanging pendent leaves prevented the rain or moisture from penetrating to the wall, contrary to all other trees which are trained for bearing fruit.

Having now, to the best of my knowledge, given statements of the various obstacles which present themselves to the paper-hanger, and the modes of overcoming them, I shall endeavour to offer the best and plainest information in my power for proceeding with hanging the different kinds of paper, and the peculiar treatment required by some of them, which will be found noticed under each head; but, first, I hope it will not be considered impertinent in me to offer a few observations on general principles to be observed in paper-hanging; and I do so the more confidently from the conviction that they are not invariably attended to, although, it will be granted, attention to them is indispensable in perfecting the work; for instance, many striped or other formal patterns require uniformity in the several compartments of a room, especially in that part immediately over the chimney-piece; and although such like patterns may be unsuitable where pictures are to be hung, yet there is no accounting for taste in such cases, and therefore it is the business of the workman to make it his constant practice to follow the rule of uniformity.

Another part of practice should be invariably adhered to,—all overlapping joints should face the light as much as is practicable, for although paper is thin, yet it will cast a shadow sufficiently to render the joining more discernible, consequently a fault to be avoided; and this may be done by cutting the edges of the paper on the contrary sides, and in breadths, in number correspondent to answer the termination where the meeting may be the least objectionable.

There are two ways I have adopted, so that the pattern may be uniform over the chimney-pieces; one or the other of them, according to circumstances, was always satisfactory: the first is, if you are desirous to begin a part of the room distant from the chimney-piece, cut slips across the piece exactly the breadth, with sufficient of the pattern on each for observation;

paste them, then place the slips in uniformity over the chimney-piece, and continue them to where you intend to commence; thus you will find the *part of the pattern* you must begin with, whether it may chance to be a more or less part of your first breadth. This method, which is attended with little trouble or loss of time, will, if carefully set out, bring you to your object with close nicety.

My other method is, presuming you purpose to observe what I have before noticed, relating to the overlapping edge of the paper being kept to the light, to begin over the chimney-piece in uniformity, leaving the overlapping edge a little raised, and so with each breadth, that you can slip the succeeding one underneath, till you arrive at the terminating part you fix upon.

I need not say much on the manner of cutting the edges of the paper, as the slovenly practice of cutting one edge only is now laid aside; some paper-hangers cut the overlapping edge only before pasting, leaving the other to be taken off afterward by the person pasting, after it is pasted and doubled over: this method is easy of accomplishment, if the paster can be relied upon in doubling over the breadth; but a clever paper-hanger would in general leave no time for the paster to perform that part of the operation. I prefer cutting *both edges* before commencement, as that which has to be undermost can be cut exactly to what I wish, viz:—leaving on only a very little for the other to lap over, and which in thin delicate papers is indispensable, as is also *cleanliness* in pasting. To this end I have found that carefully laying the breadths evenly, with the overlapping edges about an inch from that side of the table where the paster is situated, and bringing the piece which is pasting *just* to the front edge, not only conduces to cleanliness, but renders the doubling over more easy and expeditious. I hope I may be excused adding

some concluding remarks in this department
of the business, from having observed what
I *consider* an *irregular* mode, of proceeding.
I shall not intrude further in explaining it,
but state mine, leaving others to judge of
its propriety.

Having laid my breadths evenly one over
the other, as before observed, I place them
so that about as much of them may hang
over one end of the table as the other, and
having the vessel containing the paste on
the floor at my right hand, I draw the
breadth along the table till the end of the
breadth is even with the *left* end of the
table, where I begin pasting from the left
to the right; the paper is then doubled
over, and passed to the left, to finish the
breadth.

The paster should observe to fold the
breadth so that the paper-hanger may have
the longest part to commence with, at the
top of the room, for the obvious reason,
that of affording better means of placing

5*

the breadth plumb, and matching the pattern: this is easily effected by a little attention on the part of the person who is pasting, viz:—if the hanging of the paper is going from right to left, let the first fold be the longest; and if from left to right, the shortest; as the overlapping edge is always next to him, it accounts for the intended purpose.

I have the pleasure of acknowledging my gratitude and indebtedness for the greatest part of the preceding articles to the instructions of one of the most clever and expeditious paper-hangers I ever met with, and with whom I served a regular apprenticeship: after a practice of upward of fifty years, a better system has not been presented to me; and I trust it may be as satisfactory to others.

The respected person I have alluded to has been deceased many years, since which, with paper-hanging, as with other businesses, many changes have taken place, calling for

frequent observations, which I flatter myself I have in some degree regarded: such
as they are, they will be found in the succeeding part of this treatise.

Lining Paper.

LINING paper is in most cases to be recommended as a ground for delicate paper-hangings; it adds much to a soft effect, as also causing an evenness on the wall, and a quicker absorption of the paste, the want of which is frequently injurious to the finer colours; to stained grounds it is inadmissible. As this kind of paper is now made in webs of considerable length at the mill, it is found to afford more advantages both in neatness and expedition than formerly, when it was only procurable in sheets. At present no more is required than to cut the length from the web, the sides being straight and even, so that it can be hung vertically without further preparation; such breadths of lining paper, as also all cross joinings, must invariably be put on close, *without the least overlapping*.

When the paper is put up and *quite* dry, any small knots or inequalities may be taken off by slightly rubbing them with a flat piece of pumice-stone; but this must be used carefully, so that no slivers may be raised, as such defects would be visible upon the paper which has to go over it.

If the lining paper has to precede a crimson or scarlet *stained ground* paper, *alum* must on no account be an ingredient in the paste, but in this case use No. 2 paste.

I have before mentioned sponge as one of the requisites for paper-hanging; it is frequently omitted, although *indispensable* in regard to cleanliness in taking off spots or daubs of wet paste while hanging the paper. Moisten a clean soft sponge in clean cold water, *dab* the spot with it, but by no means rub it: by observing this, the sponge may be used upon the most delicate paper with proper effect, as will be seen on its becoming dry; otherwise the mark will be visible on a side view.

India Paper.

THE demand for this beautiful kind of paper, vying with the richest colours in nature, was always, from its great value, confined to palaces and mansions of this country; and the great improvements in the English and French paper-hangings have rendered that demand still less, so that, at present, the paper-hanger is scarcely called upon to hang it; and few observations are needed respecting it. The fabric being made of brittle materials, and the breadth of the paper considerable, great care is required in handling it: except this, the hanging of it is easy and agreeable, as the colours are not liable to be moved by the moisture of the paste. In some of these papers the breadths are numbered consecutively, but it seldom happens that the patterns are so correct as to match them with exactness: to remedy such defects, it is usual to cut out neatly a sprig, small bird, or butterfly, as the case may be, to form a kind of communication, so as to be agreeable to the eye. In regard to borders for India paper, I can only say I have *seen* them of the same materials, suitable to the richness of the colours of the papers, but none have come under my hands. I have therefore put up burnished gold mouldings, inclining to narrow and plain kinds, which I have found gave satisfaction.

It is not my intention to enter into a dissertation on taste; for however correct may be that of the paper-hanger, it must give way, and that very properly, to that of his employer; yet his suggestions are frequently acceptable; and, in the hope that mine may not be out of order, I shall venture occasionally to offer them in this treatise, as they occur to my mind.

I first beg to refer to a practice, which has long been general, that of fitting the

paper close to all the terminating parts of a
room, without adding any kind of border,
leaving an unfinished appearance; and this
system has continued for such a great
length of time, that the younger part of the
present generation seldom know the effect
of a border, it being a stranger to their eye-
sight, they are incompetent to judge by
comparison.   On this particular subject I
do not hesitate to substitute opinion in lieu
of suggestion, as, I think, by some modification, deviating from the old mode of putting
on borders of preposterous breadth about
every part where they could with any propriety apply it.   I admit that a change was
required, and likely to take place, as better
taste advanced; but why should borders be
entirely discarded? thus passing to a contrary extreme.   I presume some influential
leader of fashion of extreme sensibility and
super-refined taste, with perhaps the addition of a spice of economy, effected the
opposing change.

It is my humble opinion that borders ought to be used invariably, under the modification I have alluded to, since the chaste style in which they are now brought out especially qualifies them for any required effect.

The mode I would recommend, as a medium between the extremes of ancient and modern practice, is, to apply borders, in all cases, to the tops and bottoms of apartments that are papered. I readily allow that, for small rooms, where there are several doorways, borders may be dispensed with; but even for these small rooms, selections of borders might be made, to give an improved effect. I shall mention one sort, among several others of a like description, for the purpose,—that one in imitation of gimp, about an inch broad, which is to be had at most paper-hanging establishments.

In advocating the invariable use of borders for the tops and bottoms of rooms, I venture to presume that my sentiments are borne out comparatively, on the acknowledged principles of correct architecture; for instance, how defective would a column appear without its capital? as also without its basement, with the exception of the Doric; and in that it is omitted only for the sake of convenience, to accommodate crowded assemblages.

On the Hanging of Flock Papers with Crimson Stained Grounds.

I BELIEVE it will be allowed by practical men in the trade, that in hanging this kind of paper, more care and attention are required than in the case of any other; therefore I hope an explanation of the method I adopt may not be unacceptable.

These *crimson stained grounds* are subject, from even trifling mismanagement, to be discoloured, such as using paste in which *alum* is an ingredient; it changes the crimson to a dingy purple. A super-abundance of a proper paste will also have a bad effect; therefore, this, and unnecessary delay in putting it up after pasting, should be avoided. I make these preliminary observations, to lead to a more clear understanding of the succeeding directions.

Pastes Nos. 2 and 4 *only*, are suitable. They must be in separate vessels, with a *brush to each*. As great adhesiveness is *only* required in the overlapping side of the breadth, that must be done with the stiff paste to the extent of from one to two inches; no more of that is required; the remaining part of the breadth may be quickly passed over with paste No. 2, observing *particularly* that the brush with *this paste* does not come to the extreme edge, as passing over the strong paste would reduce its adhesiveness, the thing most desirable.

The advantages of this system of using two sorts of paste will be obvious to a practical paper-hanger. He knows that this kind of paper does not require a quantity of strong or other paste, except what I have mentioned. Expedition is the next consideration to which this method conduces; not only as regards the time of the workman, but likewise preventing the necessity of much rubbing with the brush in distributing the paste over the breadth, when it is of an *unnecessarily strong* consistence, with the risk of steeping the paper beyond a proper state for hanging it.

All *cross-joints* must be very cleanly cut with a straight edge and a sharp knife; the edges of the paper to jump against each other, without the least over-lapping, (and so of *other* flock papers.) Lining paper is indispensable, as by its absorption of the paste, the upper one dries more readily.

The next thing to attend to in this, (as in all other flock embossed papers,) is to take off with a sharp knife the little pips, or marks of flock occasioned by the setting on of the printing blocks, as also any small inequalities of flock projecting beyond the pattern, which is sometimes the case. These imperfections appear small, but if not removed, they repel the edge which has to be laid over them, and give much trouble in the hanging.

Burnished gold moulding is the most

suitable border, generally, for this paper; but I have seen a wood moulding, upon a dining-room, harmonize very well with it; it was about two inches broad; a small bead at each edge, and a *plain* fillet between them japanned a rich morone colour, the beads darker than the centre, and corresponding with the darkest tint of the flock.

Crimson ground paper, such as I have mentioned, with a small figure of flock, corresponding in tone of colour with the ground, has a fine effect where several gold frames are upon it. When this is not the case, crimson flock papers, unless richly heightened with bronze or gold, give to an apartment a sombre appearance, which the strongest light can scarcely remove.

Panelling.

FOR the effect, in the panelling of an apartment, much depends upon taste; and frequently the style is directed by the employer. Still, the workman, in case of his being appealed to, should, from his experience, be enabled to explain the mode best adapted for producing the desired effect of elegance. I shall, therefore, limit myself to a few observations and suggestive hints.

Where the fireplace, doors, and windows are situated uniformly in an apartment, there is little difficulty in deciding upon the mode of proceeding: for, should it be spacious, the first object regards the proportions, in breadth, of the styles and rails, (carpentry terms,) which govern the size and effect of the panels, which are presumed to be regular in each compartment.

The styles and rails are generally of one
chaste colour; they, with the panels, should
harmonize with the general tone of colour
observable in the furniture. If a degree of
splendour is required, it will be effected by
forming the panels with burnished gold
mouldings and angle ornaments; the outer-
most moulding rich, the inner one, forming
the panel, small and chaste.

Another mode of panelling is sometimes
preferred, and by persons of acknowledged
good taste; that of forming each of the
sides and ends of the room into one entire
panel. In cases where the fireplace, doors,
&c. are irregularly situated, this method is
the only one of making the panelling unobjectionable.

Elegant panelling may be effected by
using paper borders and angle ornaments:
they are now brought out by the paper-
stainers in every variety suitable for the
purpose.

In all compartments of a panelled room,

the greatest nicety should be observed in centring the pattern in the panels; for, if pictures have to be placed in them, the least deviation from uniformity will be perceptible, and also displeasing to the eye. Regard should be paid to keeping the overlapping edges of the paper toward the light, for the reason before stated.

Directions for Preparing and Hanging an Apartment with Printed Cotton.

THERE are two departments in this operation: the first by the paper-hanger, the other in the way of upholstery. As the business of the paper-hanger has precedence, he may, as I have been, be expected to superintend the completion. I, therefore, insert the detail of the entire operation, presuming it may, in like cases, be acceptable.

Should there be any appearance of damp upon the walls which are to be covered, the whole, or such parts of the room as are affected, must be battened and canvassed, in the manner before described, (No. 2, on the Preparation of Rooms,) and removing all knots from the canvas; it is then to be hung neatly with lining paper, so that it may form a perfectly smooth ground for the cotton. It must be observed, in cases where rooms are only partially damp, as to require battens and canvas, that the remaining parts, which are dry, must have all, even the least, protuberances taken off; and battens must be let in flush with the face of the wall, at the top, bottom, round the doors, windows, and *double* at the angles; on which the cotton has to be fixed with *tinned* tacks. Lining paper over all the walls is indispensable.

Where an entire room is free from damp, the like treatment is requisite.

Such is the paper-hanger's department; and supposing he has undertaken the completion of the work, he must superintend it. I would recommend him to engage an upholsterer as his assistant, and proceed as follows.

As cotton for this purpose is generally highly glazed, the straining of it is, at the best, rather difficult upon large compartments, mostly an entire side or end of a room; and when properly managed, must be free from fold, crease, or wrinkle.

The paper-hanger will attend to the preparation of the breadths which have to be joined, so that the pattern matches as well as printed cotton will allow. The *selvages must* now be torn off; and, I must add, this is *indispensable* in effecting the requisite straining; about a quarter of an inch taken off will be sufficient, unless the matching of the pattern requires more. The breadths are now to be arranged consecutively for the compartments, and each numbered, for the sempstress; who must be especially cautioned to avoid crumpling or creasing it, and to sew it very evenly in backstitch with good *double* silk of a suitable colour: for, observe, if the stitches break out in straining, there is no means of repairing it without taking it down from the wall.

The breadths being put together for each compartment, as directed, attend to the uniform centring of the pattern, as in paper, for the reasons before given; then proceed by beginning at the top in the centre, and form the cotton in its place *slightly* by pins or tacks, so that it is observed to be properly arranged, by placing all the centres of the top, bottom, and sides exactly, as all the straining should proceed from these points; those from the top to the bottom having precedence; and be particular that, in drawing the cotton, it is pulled in a direct line with the tack you are driving, as the *least* twisting of the high glazed cotton would mar the business.

The most proper tacks for the purpose are the fine eight-ounce tinned sort, and they are required to be rather close to each other; the nailing to be about an inch from the extremities, and the edges of the cotton pasted down.

By adopting carefully the means I have laid down, a job of a rather particular description will, I doubt not, be accomplished

7

to the satisfaction of both workman and employer.

As a border or finish to the foregoing, a round soft flossed worsted rope, in shades suitable to the cotton, has a good effect. It must be of a substance to cover the tacks, and will be required to be double at the angles: the rope is fixed with brads. Burnished gold, or japanned mouldings, are also suitable.

N. B.—If the pattern of the cotton is incomplete at the joinings of the breadths, it is not a very difficult matter to touch up the places with water colours.

Colouring in Distemper.

THE business of a colourist is not always combined with that of a paper-hanger: nevertheless some knowledge of colouring in distemper is almost indispensable, if only for the sake of convenience. In the country, it frequently happens that a professed colourist is not at hand; in such cases, if the paper-hanger is enabled to distemper a ceiling, either white or tinted, or the styles, &c. in panelling, then does a degree of knowledge in that department prove an advantage; and I trust that the few hints I offer may tend to such convenience.

I believe it is generally understood, that with a judicious admixture of the primitive colours, red, blue, yellow, and white, any tint can be produced, especially the various shades and tints of drabs, which are commonly most in demand; and for colouring in distemper, the native earths and ochres are generally sufficient, except for delicate purposes, when the finer colours, such as scarlet, crimson, purple, and yellow lakes, and some others, are requisite.

The various blue and green verditors are suitable for distemper colouring; the Dutch and rose pinks are sometimes used, but they cannot be relied upon in water-colouring.

The colour called French gray is prepared by a composition of ball or Spanish white and indigo, the latter being finely ground upon a stone; but from the difficulty, by this method, of reducing it to a proper state, it is advisable to add water, and strain it through flannel upon the whiting, till the required tint is obtained.

Some of the common earths and ochres are gritty, and require washing over, which is the best way to obtain them pure; but this being troublesome, they are generally ground upon a painter's stone.

I have, under the head of "sizing for walls," observed that buffalo spetches produce the best size; and the proper consistence for distemper is a weak trembling jelly in a *cold state*. If the heat of the atmosphere, or other causes, reduces it to a fluid state, it will be improper, as the colour would then, instead of being suspended in the size, fall to the bottom of the vessel containing it, which should on no account be suffered; therefore the vessel should be kept in a cool place or cellar in summer, till the moment it is wanted. I may further observe, that in hot weather, the proper consistence or strength of the size cannot be ascertained unless it is put into a cool place. I am thus particular relating to it, as I consider it an essential toward perfection in the operation.

The colour must be mixed with cold water to the tint desired, in proper quantity *at once*, and of *rather* stiff consistence; add sufficient size to complete the work, stir

7*

them well together and pass them through a strainer. If properly done, the composition will be of the consistence of thick cream, keeping the colour in suspension while using it.

The brushes for large work, in distemper, are the three-knotted ground hogs' hair sort: few others are required. In laying on the colour, the practice till of late years was to lay it evenly, one way only; the present method is to pass the brush in every indiscriminate direction, and leaving it in that state, which it is considered gives it a more solid appearance. A more recent method for obtaining the like object is called stippling, by means of a large, stiff, hogs'-hair brush, with a perfect flat face, and a conveniently formed handle.

APPENDIX.

APPENDIX.

WHEN I commenced this Treatise, it was my intention to confine the subject entirely to the practical part of paper-hanging, with its precedent preparations only. Since that time, some persons, judging from my long experience, suggested to me that I might add some observations which might be acceptable in upholstery, with which I was equally conversant. In accordance with their suggestions, I shall in these additions attempt such as I trust may be useful to those inexperienced, if not important to older practitioners.

My experience extending to the latter end of the last century; perhaps, a retrospective glance at the various styles in use at the several periods since that time, may not be out of place; showing the progress, and cause of improvement, to the present day. From such early experience, I am enabled to remark, that at the beginning and up to the middle of the last century, papered rooms were only to be found in the houses of the opulent; and, judging from the papers I have had to remove to replace with others, those I found printed upon a ground unprepared in distemper; the patterns, large bold scrolls, plain and embossed, generally in blue, upon a self-drab ground. Such as these preceded those in use at the time I first knew any thing of the business.

Upholstery, at this period, toward the latter end of the last century, was very plain and simple, with the exception of the noble, massive, and canopied state beds, with formal silk damask hangings, and the walls of the rooms hung with the same kind of material, with gold mouldings. India cabinets, and other splendid antique furniture, added a grandeur to such rooms, which has not been exceeded in modern times.

At a still later period, the English paper-hangings were limited both in quality and design; the grounds of the commoner kind coarse in the extreme; the heavy duty charged upon them acting as a considerable bar to competition or improvement.

Articles in upholstery were also very plain; moreens were in general use; and I may remark that they were *really* moreens, and not the common watered, narrow, flimsy stuff that is now passed off falsely under that name. The beds were made up with plain valances, with scrolls of lace; and the window-curtains drawn up to laths, with cord, forming festoons. In the best apartments, beautiful chintzes were frequently used; the furniture, mostly of mahogany, was plain, with little claim to elegance, and the mode of stuffing the seats of chairs, &c. was equally simple.

The period of the French revolution
opened a new era in the style of furnishing. To Morell was owing the introduction
of a complete change in every department
of it: that of the French paper-hangings
were not quite accordant to English taste,
yet the English manufacturers availed themselves of the example, as regarded the su-
perior chasteness of their grounds; and the
taste of the paper-hanger was brought into
exercise, for the first time, by the panelling
of rooms. The upholsterer, also, had still
greater call for ingenuity: the elegant di-
versified French draperies, their mode of
stuffing, and the complete change from the
English practice, required more than ordinary ability in the workman; but perse-
verance and a spirit of emulation were not
wanting to complete success.

About the same time, it is due to the
Echarts of Chelsea, to notice that they commenced with a speculation which evinced
a spirit of enterprise, deserving of better

success than it met with,—that of painting arabesque upon satin, by the first artists; but it was too expensive even for that day of general patronage to suchlike arts.

The French style, in some degree, may be said to exist at the present time, but it has occasionally had to give way to particular circumstances; as, for instance, on the naval victory of the Nile, paper-hangings, cottons, brass, and wood-work in furniture, were nearly all Egyptian, with crocodiles and other inhabitants of the Nile. These were things so unattractive, not to say repulsive, that they were very pleasingly superseded by the Grecian style, which, from its lightness and elegance, is difficult, and perhaps undesirable to supplant, as regards tasteful productions.

The paper-hangings of the present day,—thanks to the removal of the heavy duty upon them—prove what can be done when the manufacturers are untrammelled; whether we look to the elegance of design, the chasteness of colouring, or the richness of those embossed and illuminated by gold and bronze; all these combine to call forth due admiration of English taste and enterprise.

In upholstery, the Grecian round and soft stuffing has superseded the square and hard stuffing of the French, which was more calculated for the display of medallions and rich borders than ease and comfort. I hope to be excused for this digression, and shall now revert to the proposed observations.

Although the hanging of walls with printed cotton is more the business of the upholsterer than the paper-hanger, it will be found, in this treatise, addressed to the latter; and the reason why it was so, is there explained, which I hope will be a sufficient apology; but now that I am entering somewhat into upholstery, I recommend it to the attention of the upholsterer, being analogous to several other parts of the business. For instance, in canvassing a room preparatory to papering, the centre at the top is the place to commence with the nailing; and in proceeding, to observe keeping the canvas square, by the weft and woof being at right angles. In the stuffing of sofas and seats, the same principle should be observed; and although it may appear a simple recommendation, I have noticed it frequently neglected, and ultimately attended with much trouble to completion.

I have already explained the reason of exceeding my original intention; and to carry out this object, it is necessary for me to revert to some things previously but slightly touched upon, especially in the decorative department of the trades.

As regards the situation of rooms in a mansion, the purpose of their use generally determines their suitable aspect. For instance, the dining-room toward the north, and occupied in the evening, requires every thing to give it the effect of warmth and comfort. For this room few ornaments are requisite, beyond the display on the sideboard, the walls coloured in distemper, or painted flat in oil, of a warm colour, with gold or japanned mouldings: panelling in imitation of oak is also appropriate; the curtains claret or crimson cloth, trimmed with gold-coloured orris lace, a brass rod with a plain fringed valance, or a valance alone, are sufficiently genteel, observing that the valance is well wadded to intercept the light. A Turkey carpet is most suitable, and, from its durability, economical; but the Axminster or Brussels, in suitable colours, are very good substitutes. The doors and other wood work in imitation of oak. The furniture in a dining-room, such as sideboard, &c., are more in the province of the cabinet than the upholstery department, and with such it is not my intention to interfere further than I find necessary for occasional explanation.

THE DRAWING-ROOM

Should have a warmer aspect than the foregoing, although generally used for evening parties; the arrangements, consequently, require much taste and judgment, so that, in their disposal, the whole may be in perfect harmony. The walls panelled with watered silk, of pearl white, or *light* tints of pink, or lavender; the styles of the same ground as the panels, painted or embroidered in arabesque; a narrow burnished gold bead, or moulding, separating the panels and styles; and a rich ogee or reeded outer moulding, with suitable carved corners, in burnished gold. But the improvement in paper-hangings, of late years, has caused little occasion for silk in panelling, as every richness and effect are accomplished in a manner equally pleasing, and in such variety as to satisfy the most fastidious taste; and what has been recommended in silk

8*

may be substituted by paper, with the like effect, as every appropriate ornament, pilasters, &c. are to be procured, of the richest description.

In rooms which are spacious and lofty, the hangings should be light, yet ample, with fine, flowing drapery: the material silk tabaret, or damask, and of a colour to harmonize with the walls of the room. If the panels are white satin, light blue hangings will be pleasing, with rich fringe, and trimmings to correspond. Under-curtains of muslin, with daisy fringe, add much to the effect in softening the light, where the windows are large or numerous. The cornices, in burnished gold. For lining to the curtains, the stuff called tammy is preferable to calico.

In drawing-rooms which are confined or low, a light-grounded chintz, of a small pattern, lined with light blue, or light apple green, is genteel, and of cheerful effect; the fringe in colour to correspond. Where the

space between the top of the window
architrave and the cornice of the room is
small, a rich plummetted worsted fringe
valance may be preferred to drapery; this
valance, of a semicircular form, to hang
deep at the sides, with silk drops, at inter-
vals of six or eight inches; the length of
the drops varied, according to the part they
fall upon the fringe, so as to be even with
the bottom of it. For windows which are
wide, instead of being semicircular, it may
be advisable to make the valances pointed
in the centre; in either case, the worsted
platt should be rather firm, about the thickness of a small finger, and in depth at the
narrowest part nine to ten inches, and at
the sides, eighteen to twenty inches: a
wadded valance of the same shape, at the
back to intercept the light, is required: the
cornices gold, or gold and japan. This
style has been much approved by persons
of acknowledged taste. The mode of loop-
ing up window curtains should be rather

low than high in all cases, but more particularly in low rooms; and the curtains, when so looped, should be of a length to hang gracefully upon the floor.

In the choice of carpets, much depends upon a proper selection for giving effect to the furniture placed upon them. From my observations, I am of opinion they should not be in colours too attractive, so as to draw the attention from other objects; rather let them be considered neutral grounds, yet not deficient in richness.

In painting the wood-work of the room, French white, or chaste tints, answering to those in the panels, if such are preferred to French white, with the mouldings in gold, and imitation of bird's-eye maple, is suitable. Satin-wood is too flat for effect.

THE LADY'S BOUDOIR

May be decorated much in the same style as the drawing-room, but in every respect of a lighter description: ladies generally display their taste in ornamenting it with drawings, and other articles, the productions of themselves, or friends. Light blue satin paper panels are calculated to give effect to gold frames, observing that the figure of it is small, with little contrast to the ground of the paper.

Muslin curtains alone, tastefully put up, or pearl-white damask, with trimmings in silk of the same, are handsome and suitable for this room.

THE LIBRARY,

Being a room of much consequence, the furnishing of it should be rich and bold, if the room is spacious and lofty. In libraries where the bookcases do not occupy considerable space, panelling may be introduced with good effect, as may also pilasters, of a chaste description. If pictures are to be placed in the panels, these may be of a crimson flock paper, the pattern small, without gold or bronze: should there be no pictures, in that case crimson flock papers require heightening with gold or bronze, as without such embellishment they are dark in an evening without strong candlelight. As a general observation, a library paper should be more inclined to grave than gay; the moulding gold, or oak and gold.

The hangings to the windows should be rich and ample; purple, or claret-coloured silk velvet, are splendid beyond any other material; their lustre by candlelight has a magnificent effect; the fringe orris lace border, and trimmings silk of a gold colour. The cornices classical and bold, in oak and gold.

I may here remark, that every kind of cornice, borders, and other ornaments, are to be procured in papier-maché, of the most beautiful description, classical, antique, and modern.

BED-ROOMS.

In the best apartments paper-hangings are generally selected chaste and handsome, with satin grounds, the figures in subdued colours, yet to harmonize with the hangings; the borders, at top and bottom of the rooms, of paper, unless India paper is used; in that case, gold moulding. I have to notice the prevalence, of late years, in leaving out borders entirely to papered rooms. This arose from two motives, viz. economy and the previous use of extravagant heavy broad borders, which certainly were too preposterous to continue in favour: these causes led to an extreme change, by borders being excluded altogether. This erroneous style is now corrected, persons of acknowledged taste adopting those chaste embossed kinds, such as are in imitation of gimp, shaded lines, moulding, &c., for giving a finishing effect to the tops and bottoms of papered rooms, the paper being fitted close to the sides of doors and windows.

The materials suitable for hangings to bed-rooms are so various, it is needless to particularize them, further than that those for the family use may be of highly glazed chintz, of which we have now many beautiful patterns, or of damask, or morone; the colours, crimson, barre, deep yellow, and light morone: these give a warm effect to the apartments: light green and blue are also frequently used. The fitting up of these apartments may be plain, but full and handsome; if moreen is the material, folded valances are applicable, in preference to drapery: but damask being soft and pliable, it is well adapted to form any drapery that may be desired. Silk fringe and trimmings, in the same colours, are quite as elegant, and more tasty, if not so showy, as contrasts.

STATE ROOMS.

In those state rooms set apart for visitors, there is much scope for the display of taste: silk damask, or rich chintz, are most suitable; the former lined with fine light stuff; the latter with pink, light blue, green, or morone highly-glazed calico: morone silk quality binding harmonizes with any of them; as does also drab plumetted fringe of worsted with varied silk hangers. Drapery is indispensable for these rooms; and their style of elegance depends upon the taste of the upholsterer, whose practical knowledge enables him to adopt the most pleasing forms for the purposes to which they are to be applied; but economy, as with unbordered papered rooms, was the cause of drapery being superseded by home-made folded valances, which a tailor, a mantua-maker, or housekeeper, with the maid-servants, while on board wages, could manage, as no art or taste was required. However, at the present time, with the proper exceptions already mentioned, in the material of moreen, draperies, and elegant ones too, now prevail, as much as they did at the time of their introduction by Morell. I may mention a mode of trimming which has a good effect, viz. turning over the lining upon the chintz to the breadth of an inch or more, and cording the edge where they meet.

An alcove in a bed-room is a great acquisition to it, as affording an opportunity of displaying much taste in fitting up. For instance, should the height of the room allow it, the bed may be elevated upon a dais, raised by one or two steps from the floor of the room; the entire inside of the alcove fluted from top to bottom, in glazed calico, the same as the bed: rose colour, overlaid with muslin or net, has a chaste effect; the counterpane in the like manner, and fringed as the bed: a light muslin or net drapery round the top of the alcove, is a beautiful finish to it; the bed with canopy, tasteful , light drapery; and a suitable maché cornice completes the interior. For the exterior, or entrance to the alcove, there is usually a space from the top of it to the cornice of the room; this space may have a fringed drapery to correspond, and to range with the top of the alcove, whatever may be its shape; the window curtains also suitable.

Carpets, entirely covering bed-rooms, impart a comfortable effect; but some families object to it; but whenever carpets are used either way in bed-rooms, I particularly recommend French casters to the bedsteads.

There are many other minor articles in upholstery; but they are so well known to the trade, that to treat of them would be superfluous. I shall only add an ex-tract from my former publication, " An Analysis of Drapery," wherein I gave a

tabular scale for the various sizes of festoons, or as they are sometimes denomi-
nated by the trade " swags."

I have designedly refrained from trench-
ing upon the cabinet-maker's department,
except where I found it necessary to eluci-
date my subject; and having already explained the reason of my exceeding my
original intention, and to carry out this
object, I have found it necessary to revert
to some things previously but slightly
touched upon; but in enlarging my treatise, I have studiously abstained from the
ideal; by long experience, from practice,
in furnishing for the first families, added
to by observations from those persons in
the trade, of acknowledged taste, I am
emboldened to presume my efforts in this
publication may be candidly and favour-
ably appreciated; and with this apology I
beg to conclude.

EXPLANATION

TO THE TABLE OF FESTOONS.

(*P.* 103 *to* 108.)

IT may readily be conceived from such a number, varying in size, as is given in the following Table, that, by combination, a drapery may be formed over windows and piers of a room to any required extent; a little attention by a person of taste will enable him to form a pleasing drapery, by selecting such sizes as are desirable, and passing one or both folded ends over the cornice, and again others underneath, so that they appear twisted over the cornice connectedly.

Plate 2 shows the manner of continuing the festoons to any extent, as also the shape of the suspended drapery at the side, which may be enlarged or reduced, observing the like proportions.

Extreme extent required for the festoon, when fitted up.	Depth required for the festoon to hang, when fitted up.	The given size for the bottom of festoon: see diagram.	The given size for the top of festoon: see diagram.	The side which the ends are to be folded to: see diagram.
ft. in.	ft. in.	ft. in.	ft. in.	in.
6 6	4 0	11 4½	5 8	9·
6 0	" "	10 11	4 3	"
5 6	" "	10 7	4 10	"
5 0	" "	10 4	4 4	"
4 6	" "	10 1	4 4	6
4 0	" "	9 10	3 11	"
3 6	" "	9 7	3 6	"
3 0	" "	9 4	3 1	"
2 6	" "	9 1	2 9	"
2 0	" "	8 11	2 6	"
6 6	3 9	10 11	5 8	9
6 0	" "	10 7½	5 3	"
5 6	" "	10 4	4 10	"
5 0	" "	10 1	4 4	"
4 6	" "	9 10	4 4	6
4 0	" "	9 7	3 11	"
3 6	" "	9 4	3 6	"
3 0	" "	9 1	3 1	"
2 6	" "	8 10	2 9	"
2 0	" "	8 7	2 6	"
6 6	3 6	10 6	5 8	9
6 0	" "	10 2	5 4	"
5 6	" "	9 10	4 10	"
5 0	" "	9 6	4 4	"

Extreme extent required for the festoon, when fitted up.		Depth required for the festoon to hang, when fitted up.		The given size for the bottom of festoon: see diagram.		The given size for the top of festoon: see diagram.		The size which the ends are to be folded to: see diagram.
ft.	in.	ft.	in.	ft.	in.	ft.	in.	in.
4	6	3	6	9	2	4	4	6
4	0	"	"	8	10	3	11	"
3	6	"	"	8	7	3	6	"
3	0	"	"	8	4	3	1	"
2	6	"	"	8	2	2	9	"
2	0	"	"	8	0	2	6	"
6	6	3	3	10	2	5	8	9
6	0	"	"	9	10½	5	3	"
5	6	"	"	9	7	4	10	"
5	0	"	"	9	3½	4	4	"
4	6	"	"	9	0	4	4	6
4	0	"	"	8	9	3	11	"
3	6	"	"	8	6	3	6	"
3	0	"	"	8	3	3	1	"
2	6	"	"	8	0	2	9	"
2	0	"	"	7	9	2	6	"
6	6	3	0	9	8	5	8	9
6	0	"	"	9	4	5	3	"
5	6	"	"	9	0	4	10	"
5	0	"	"	8	8	4	1	"
4	6	"	"	8	4	4	4	6
4	0	"	"	8	1	3	11	"
3	6	"	"	7	10	3	6	"
3	0	"	"	7	7	3	1	"

Extreme extent required for the festoon, when fitted up.		Depth required for the festoon to hang, when fitted up.		The given size for the bottom of festoon: see diagram.		The given size for the top of festoon: see diagram.		The size which the ends are to be folded to: see diagram.
ft.	in.	ft.	in.	ft.	in.	ft.	in.	in.
2	6	3	0	7	4½	2	9	6
2	0	"	"	7	2	2	6	"
6	6	2	9	9	4	5	8	9
6	0	"	"	9	0	5	3	"
5	6	"	"	8	8	4	10	"
5	0	"	"	8	4	4	4	"
4	6	"	"	8	0	4	4	6
4	0	"	"	7	8	3	11	"
3	6	"	"	7	4½	3	0	"
3	0	"	"	7	1	3	1	"
2	6	"	"	6	10	2	9	"
2	0	"	"	6	7	2	6	"
6	6	2	6	9	0	5	8	9
6	0	"	"	8	7	5	3	"
5	6	"	"	8	3	4	10	"
5	0	"	"	7	11	4	4	"
4	6	"	"	7	7	4	4	6
4	0	"	"	7	0	3	11	"
3	6	"	"	6	11	3	6	"
3	0	"	"	6	7¾	3	1	"
2	6	"	"	6	4½	2	9	"
2	0	"	"	6	1½	2	6	"
6	6	2	3	8	8	5	8	9
6	0	"	"	8	3	5	3	"

Extreme extent required for the festoon, when fitted up.		Depth required for the festoon to hang, when fitted up.		The given size for the bottom of festoon: see diagram.		The given size for the top of festoon: see diagram.		The side which the ends are to be folded to: see diagram.
ft.	in.	ft.	in.	ft.	in.	ft.	in.	in.
5	6	2	3	7	10½	4	10	9
5	0	,,	,,	7	5½	4	4	,,
4	6	,,	,,	7	1	4	4	6
4	0	,,	,,	6	8½	3	11	,,
3	6	,,	,,	6	5	3	6	,,
3	0	,,	,,	6	1½	3	1	,,
2	6	,,	,,	5	10½	2	9	,,
2	0	,,	,,	5	7½	2	6	,,
6	6	2	0	8	4	5	8	9
6	0	,,	,,	7	11	5	3	,,
5	6	,,	,,	7	6	4	10	,,
5	0	,,	,,	7	1	4	4	,,
4	6	,,	,,	6	8½	4	4	6
4	0	,,	,,	6	4½	3	11	,,
3	6	,,	,,	6	1	3	6	,,
3	0	,,	,,	5	9½	3	1	,,
2	6	,,	,,	5	6	2	9	,,
2	0	,,	,,	5	2½	2	6	,,
1	6	,,	,,	4	11	2	2	,,
6	6	1	9	8	0	5	8	9
6	0	,,	,,	7	7	5	3	,,
5	6	,,	,,	7	2	4	10	,,
5	0	,,	,,	6	9	4	4	,,
4	6	,,	,,	6	4½	4	4	6

Extreme extent required for the festoon, when fitted up.		Depth required for the festoon to hang, when fitted up.		The given size for the bottom of festoon: see diagram.		The given size for the top of festoon: see diagram.		The size which the ends are to be folded to: see diagram.
ft.	in.	ft.	in.	ft.	in.	ft.	in.	in.
4	0	1	9	6	0	3	11	6
3	6	"	"	5	7½	3	6	"
3	0	"	"	5	3	3	1	"
2	6	"	"	4	11½	2	9	"
2	0	"	"	4	8	2	6	"
1	6	"	"	4	5½	2	2	"
6	6	1	6	7	9	5	8	9
6	0	"	"	7	3¼	5	3	"
5	6	"	"	6	10	4	10	"
5	0	"	"	6	5	4	4	"
4	6	"	"	6	0	4	4	6
4	0	"	"	5	7	3	11	"
3	6	"	"	5	2½	3	6	"
3	0	"	"	4	10	3	1	"
2	6	"	"	4	6½	2	9	"
2	0	"	"	4	3	2	6	"
1	6	"	"	4	0	2	2	"
6	6	1	3	7	6	5	8	9
6	0	"	"	7	0	5	3	"
5	6	"	"	6	6½	4	10	"
5	0	"	"	6	1	4	4	"
4	6	"	"	5	8	4	4	6
4	0	"	"	5	3	3	11	"
3	6	"	"	4	10	3	6	"

Extreme extent required for the festoon, when fitted up.		Depth required for the festoon to hang, when fitted up.		The given size for the bottom of festoon: see diagram.		The given size for the top of festoon: see diagram.		The size which the ends are to be folded to: see diagram.
ft.	in.	ft.	in.	ft.	in.	ft.	in.	in.
3	0	1	3	4	5	3	1	6
2	6	"	"	4	1	2	9	"
2	0	"	"	3	9½	2	6	"
1	6	"	"	3	6	2	2	"
4	6	1	0	5	5	4	4	6
4	0	"	"	4	11¾	3	11	"
3	6	"	"	4	6	3	6	"
3	0	"	"	4	1	3	1	"
2	6	"	"	3	9	2	9	"
2	0	"	"	3	5	2	6	"
1	6	"	"	3	1	2	2	"

THE END.

STEREOTYPED BY L. JOHNSON AND CO.
PHILADELPHIA.

CATALOGUE
OF
PRACTICAL AND SCIENTIFIC BOOKS,
PUBLISHED BY
HENRY CAREY BAIRD,
INDUSTRIAL PUBLISHER,
No. 406 WALNUT STREET,
PHILADELPHIA.

☞ Any of the Books comprised in this Catalogue will be sent by mail, free of postage, at the publication price.

☞ My New and Enlarged Catalogue, 95 pages 8vo., with full descriptions of Books, will be sent, free of postage, to any one who will favor me with his address.

ARMENGAUD, AMOUROUX, AND JOHNSON.—THE PRACTICAL DRAUGHTSMAN'S BOOK OF INDUSTRIAL DESIGN, AND MACHINIST'S AND ENGINEER'S DRAWING COMPANION: Forming a complete course of Mechanical Engineering and Architectural Drawing. From the French of M. Armengaud the elder, Prof. of Design in the Conservatoire of Arts and Industry, Paris, and MM. Armengaud the younger and Amouroux, Civil Engineers. Rewritten and arranged, with additional matter and plates, selections from and examples of the most useful and generally employed mechanism of the day. By William Johnson, Assoc. Inst. C. E., Editor of "The Practical Mechanic's Journal." Illustrated by 50 folio steel plates and 50 wood-cuts. A new edition, 4to. . $10 00

ARLOT.—A COMPLETE GUIDE FOR COACH PAINTERS.
Translated from the French of M. Arlot, Coach Painter; late Master Painter for eleven years with M. Ehrler, Coach Manufacturer, Paris. With important American additions . . $1 25

ARROWSMITH.—PAPER-HANGER'S COMPANION:
A Treatise in which the Practical Operations of the Trade are Systematically laid down: with Copious Directions Preparatory to Papering; Preventives against the Effect of Damp on Walls; the Various Cements and Pastes adapted to the Several Purposes of the Trade; Observations and Directions for the Panelling and Ornamenting of Rooms, &c. By James Arrowsmith. 12mo., cloth $1 25

BAIRD.—THE AMERICAN COTTON SPINNER, AND MANA-GER'S AND CARDER'S GUIDE:

A Practical Treatise on Cotton Spinning; giving the Dimensions and Speed of Machinery, Draught and Twist Calculations, etc.; with notices of recent Improvements: together with Rules and Examples for making changes in the sizes and numbers of Roving and Yarn. Compiled from the papers of the late ROBERT H. BAIRD. 12mo. . . . $1 50

BAKER.—LONG-SPAN RAILWAY BRIDGES:

Comprising Investigations of the Comparative Theoretical and Practical Advantages of the various Adopted or Proposed Type Systems of Construction; with numerous Formulæ and Tables. By B. Baker. 12mo. $2 00

BAKEWELL.—A MANUAL OF ELECTRICITY—PRACTICAL AND THEORETICAL:

By F. C. BAKEWELL, Inventor of the Copying Telegraph. Second Edition. Revised and enlarged. Illustrated by numerous engravings. 12mo. Cloth . . . .

BEANS.—A TREATISE ON RAILROAD CURVES AND THE LOCATION OF RAILROADS:

By E. W. BEANS, C. E. 12mo. . . . $2 00

BLENKARN.—PRACTICAL SPECIFICATIONS OF WORKS EXECUTED IN ARCHITECTURE, CIVIL AND MECHANICAL ENGINEERING, AND IN ROAD MAKING AND SEWERING:

To which are added a series of practically useful Agreements and Reports. By JOHN BLENKARN. Illustrated by fifteen large folding plates. 8vo. $9 00

BLINN.—A PRACTICAL WORKSHOP COMPANION FOR TIN, SHEET-IRON, AND COPPER-PLATE WORKERS:

Containing Rules for Describing various kinds of Patterns used by Tin, Sheet-iron, and Copper-plate Workers; Practical Geometry; Mensuration of Surfaces and Solids; Tables of the Weight of Metals, Lead Pipe, etc.; Tables of Areas and Circumferences of Circles; Japans, Varnishes, Lackers, Cements, Compositions, etc. etc. By LEROY J. BLINN, Master Mechanic. With over One Hundred Illustrations. 12mo. $2 50

BOOTH.—MARBLE WORKER'S MANUAL:

Containing Practical Information respecting Marbles in general, their Cutting, Working, and Polishing; Veneering of Marble; Mosaics; Composition and Use of Artificial Marble, Stuccos, Cements, Receipts, Secrets, etc. etc. Translated from the French by M. L. BOOTH. With an Appendix concerning American Marbles. 12mo., cloth . . $1 50

BOOTH AND MORFIT.—THE ENCYCLOPEDIA OF CHEMISTRY, PRACTICAL AND THEORETICAL:

Embracing its application to the Arts, Metallurgy, Mineralogy, Geology, Medicine, and Pharmacy. By JAMES C. BOOTH, Melter and Refiner in the United States Mint, Professor of Applied Chemistry in the Franklin Institute, etc., assisted by CAMPBELL MORFIT, author of "Chemical Manipulations," etc. Seventh edition. Complete in one volume, royal 8vo., 978 pages, with numerous wood-cuts and other illustrations. $5 00

BOWDITCH.—ANALYSIS, TECHNICAL VALUATION, PURIFICATION, AND USE OF COAL GAS:

By Rev. W. R. BOWDITCH. Illustrated with wood engravings. 8vo. $6 50

BOX.—PRACTICAL HYDRAULICS:

A Series of Rules and Tables for the use of Engineers, etc. By THOMAS BOX. 12mo. $2 50

BUCKMASTER.—THE ELEMENTS OF MECHANICAL PHYSICS:

By J. C. BUCKMASTER, late Student in the Government School of Mines; Certified Teacher of Science by the Department of Science and Art; Examiner in Chemistry and Physics in the Royal College of Preceptors; and late Lecturer in Chemistry and Physics of the Royal Polytechnic Institute. Illustrated with numerous engravings. In one vol. 12mo. . $1 50

BULLOCK.—THE AMERICAN COTTAGE BUILDER:

A Series of Designs, Plans, and Specifications, from $200 to to $20,000 for Homes for the People; together with Warming, Ventilation, Drainage, Painting, and Landscape Gardening. By JOHN BULLOCK, Architect, Civil Engineer, Mechanician, and Editor of "The Rudiments of Architecture and Building," etc. Illustrated by 75 engravings. In one vol. 8vo. $3 50

BULLOCK. — THE RUDIMENTS OF ARCHITECTURE AND BUILDING :

For the use of Architects, Builders, Draughtsmen, Machinists, Engineers, and Mechanics. Edited by JOHN BULLOCK, author of "The American Cottage Builder." Illustrated by 250 engravings. In one volume 8vo.   .   .   . $3 50

BURGH.—PRACTICAL ILLUSTRATIONS OF LAND AND MARINE ENGINES :

Showing in detail the Modern Improvements of High and Low Pressure, Surface Condensation, and Super-heating, together with Land and Marine Boilers. By N. P. BURGH, Engineer. Illustrated by twenty plates, double elephant folio, with text.
$21 00

BURGH.—PRACTICAL RULES FOR THE PROPORTIONS OF MODERN ENGINES AND BOILERS FOR LAND AND MARINE PURPOSES.

By N. P. BURGH, Engineer. 12mo.   .   .   . $2 00

BURGH.—THE SLIDE-VALVE PRACTICALLY CONSIDERED :

By N. P. BURGH, author of " A Treatise on Sugar Machinery," "Practical Illustrations of Land and Marine Engines," "A Pocket-Book of Practical Rules for Designing Land and Marine Engines, Boilers," etc. etc. etc. Completely illustrated. 12mo. $2 00

BYRN.—THE COMPLETE PRACTICAL BREWER :

Or, Plain, Accurate, and Thorough Instructions in the Art of Brewing Beer, Ale, Porter, including the Process of making Bavarian Beer, all the Small Beers, such as Root-beer, Ginger-pop, Sarsaparilla-beer, Mead, Spruce beer, etc. etc. Adapted to the use of Public Brewers and Private Families. By M. LA FAYETTE BYRN, M. D. With illustrations. 12mo. $1 25

BYRN.—THE COMPLETE PRACTICAL DISTILLER :

Comprising the most perfect and exact Theoretical and Practical Description of the Art of Distillation and Rectification; including all of the most recent improvements in distilling apparatus; instructions for preparing spirits from the numerous vegetables, fruits, etc.; directions for the distillation and preparation of all kinds of brandies and other spirits, spirituous and other compounds, etc. etc.; all of which is so simplified that it is adapted not only to the use of extensive distillers, but for every farmer, or others who may wish to engage in the art of distilling. By M. LA FAYETTE BYRN, M. D. With numerous engravings. In one volume, 12mo. $1 50

BYRNE.—POCKET BOOK FOR RAILROAD AND CIVIL ENGINEERS:

Containing New, Exact, and Concise Methods for Laying out Railroad Curves, Switches, Frog Angles and Crossings; the Staking out of work; Levelling; the Calculation of Cuttings; Embankments; Earth-work, etc. By OLIVER BYRNE. Illustrated, 18mo., full bound $1 75

BYRNE.—THE HANDBOOK FOR THE ARTISAN, MECHANIC, AND ENGINEER:

By OLIVER BYRNE. Illustrated by 185 Wood Engravings. 8vo.
$5 00

BYRNE.—THE ESSENTIAL ELEMENTS OF PRACTICAL MECHANICS:

For Engineering Students, based on the Principle of Work. By OLIVER BYRNE. Illustrated by Numerous Wood Engravings, 12mo. $3 68

BYRNE.—THE PRACTICAL METAL-WORKER'S ASSISTANT:

Comprising Metallurgic Chemistry; the Arts of Working all Metals and Alloys; Forging of Iron and Steel; Hardening and Tempering; Melting and Mixing; Casting and Founding; Works in Sheet Metal; the Processes Dependent on the Ductility of the Metals; Soldering; and the most Improved Processes and Tools employed by Metal-Workers. With the Application of the Art of Electro-Metallurgy to Manufacturing Processes; collected from Original Sources, and from the Works of Holtzapffel, Bergeron, Leupold, Plumier, Napier, and others. By OLIVER BYRNE. A New, Revised, and improved Edition, with Additions by John Scoffern, M. B , William Clay, Wm. Fairbairn, F. R. S., and James Napier. With Five Hundred and Ninety-two Engravings; Illustrating every Branch of the Subject. In one volume, 8vo. 652 pages . $7 00

BYRNE.—THE PRACTICAL MODEL CALCULATOR:

For the Engineer, Mechanic, Manufacturer of Engine Work, Naval Architect, Miner, and Millwright. By OLIVER BYRNE. 1 volume, 8vo., nearly 600 pages $4 50

BEMROSE.—MANUAL OF WOOD CARVING: With Practical Illustrations for Learners of the Art, and Original and Selected designs. By WILLIAM BEMROSE, Jr. With an Introduction by LLEWELLYN JEWITT, F. S. A., etc. With 128 Illustrations. 4to., cloth $3 00

BAIRD.—PROTECTION OF HOME LABOR AND HOME PRO-
DUCTIONS NECESSARY TO THE PROSPERITY OF THE
AMERICAN FARMER:

By HENRY CAREY BAIRD. 8vo., paper 10

BAIRD.—THE RIGHTS OF AMERICAN PRODUCERS, AND THE
WRONGS OF BRITISH FREE TRADE REVENUE REFORM.

By HENRY CAREY BAIRD. (1870) 5

BAIRD.—SOME OF THE FALLACIES OF BRITISH-FREE-TRADE
REVENUE-REFORM.

Two Letters to Prof. A. L. Perry, of Williams College, Mass. By
HENRY CAREY BAIRD. (1871.) Paper 5

BAIRD.—STANDARD WAGES COMPUTING TABLES:

An Improvement in all former Methods of Computation, so arranged that wages for days, hours, or fractions of hours, at a spe-
cified rate per day or hour, may be ascertained at a glance. By
T. SPANGLER BAIRD. Oblong folio $5 00

BAUERMAN.—TREATISE ON THE METALLURGY OF IRON.

Illustrated. 12mo. $2 50

BICKNELL'S VILLAGE BUILDER.

55 large plates. 4to. $10 00

BISHOP.—A HISTORY OF AMERICAN MANUFACTURES:

From 1608 to 1866; exhibiting the Origin and Growth of the Prin-
cipal Mechanic Arts and Manufactures, from the Earliest Colonial
Period to the Present Time; By J. LEANDER BISHOP, M. D., ED-
WARD YOUNG, and EDWIN T. FREEDLEY. Three vols. 8vo.,
$10 00

BOX.—A PRACTICAL TREATISE ON HEAT AS APPLIED TO
THE USEFUL ARTS:

For the use of Engineers, Architects, etc. By THOMAS BOX, author of "Practical Hydraulics." Illustrated by 14 plates, containing 114 figures. 12mo. $4 25

CABINET MAKER'S ALBUM OF FURNITURE:

Comprising a Collection of Designs for the Newest and Most
Elegant Styles of Furniture. Illustrated by Forty-eight Large
and Beautifully Engraved Plates. In one volume, oblong
$5 00

CHAPMAN.—A TREATISE ON ROPE-MAKING:

As practised in private and public Rope-yards, with a Description
of the Manufacture, Rules, Tables of Weights, etc., adapted to the
Trade; Shipping, Mining, Railways, Builders, etc. By ROBERT
CHAPMAN. 24mo. $1 50

CRAIK.—THE PRACTICAL AMERICAN MILLWRIGHT AND MILLER.

Comprising the Elementary Principles of Mechanics, Mechanism, and Motive Power, Hydraulics and Hydraulic Motors, Mill-dams, Saw Mills, Grist Mills, the Oat Meal Mill, the Barley Mill, Wool Carding, and Cloth Fulling and Dressing, Wind Mills, Steam Power, &c. By DAVID CRAIK, Millwright. Illustrated by numerous wood engravings, and five folding plates. 1 vol. 8vo. $5 00

CAMPIN.—A PRACTICAL TREATISE ON MECHANICAL ENGINEERING:

Comprising Metallurgy, Moulding, Casting, Forging, Tools, Workshop Machinery, Mechanical Manipulation, Manufacture of Steam-engines, etc. etc. With an Appendix on the Analysis of Iron and Iron Ores. By FRANCIS CAMPIN, C. E. To which are added, Observations on the Construction of Steam Boilers, and Remarks upon Furnaces used for Smoke Prevention; with a Chapter on Explosions. By R. Armstrong, C. E., and John Bourne. Rules for Calculating the Change Wheels for Screws on a Turning Lathe, and for a Wheel-cutting Machine. By J. LA NICCA. Management of Steel, including Forging, Hardening, Tempering, Annealing, Shrinking, and Expansion. And the Case-hardening of Iron. By G. EDE. 8vo. Illustrated with 29 plates and 100 wood engravings.

$6 00

CAMPIN.—THE PRACTICE OF HAND-TURNING IN WOOD, IVORY, SHELL, ETC.:

With Instructions for Turning such works in Metal as may be required in the Practice of Turning Wood, Ivory, etc.. Also an Appendix on Ornamental Turning. By FRANCIS CAMPIN, with Numerous Illustrations, 12mo., cloth . . $3 00

CAPRON DE DOLE.—DUSSAUCE.—BLUES AND CARMINES OF INDIGO.

A Practical Treatise on the Fabrication of every Commercial Product derived from Indigo. By FELICIEN CAPRON DE DOLE Translated, with important additions, by Professor H. DUSSAUCE. 12mo.

CAREY.—THE WORKS OF HENRY C. CAREY:

CONTRACTION OR EXPANSION? REPUDIATION OR RESUMPTION? Letters to Hon. Hugh McCulloch. 8vo. 38

FINANCIAL CRISES, their Causes and Effects. 8vo. paper 25

HARMONY OF INTERESTS; Agricultural, Manufacturing, and Commercial. 8vo., paper $1 00
Do. do. cloth . . . $1 50

LETTERS TO THE PRESIDENT OF THE UNITED STATES. Paper $1 00

MANUAL OF SOCIAL SCIENCE. Condensed from Carey's "Principles of Social Science." By KATE McKEAN. 1 vol. 12mo. $2 25

MISCELLANEOUS WORKS: comprising "Harmony of Interests," "Money," "Letters to the President," "French and American Tariffs," "Financial Crises," "The Way to Outdo England without Fighting Her," "Resources of the Union," "The Public Debt," "Contraction or Expansion," "Review of the Decade 1857—'67," "Reconstruction," etc. etc. 1 vol. 8vo., cloth $4 50

MONEY: A LECTURE before the N. Y. Geographical and Statistical Society. 8vo., paper 25

PAST, PRESENT, AND FUTURE. 8vo. . . . $2 50

PRINCIPLES OF SOCIAL SCIENCE. 8 volumes 8vo., cloth $10 00

REVIEW OF THE DECADE 1857—'67. 8vo., paper 50

RECONSTRUCTION: INDUSTRIAL, FINANCIAL, AND POLITICAL. Letters to the Hon. Henry Wilson, U. S. S. 8vo paper 50

THE PUBLIC DEBT, LOCAL AND NATIONAL. How to provide for its discharge while lessening the burden of Taxation. Letter to David A. Wells, Esq., U. S. Revenue Commission. 8vo., paper 25

THE RESOURCES OF THE UNION. A Lecture read, Dec. 1865, before the American Geographical and Statistical Society, N. Y., and before the American Association for the Advancement of Social Science, Boston . . . 50

THE SLAVE TRADE, DOMESTIC AND FOREIGN; Why it Exists, and How it may be Extinguished. 12mo., cloth $1 50

LETTERS ON INTERNATIONAL COPYRIGHT. (1867.)
Paper 50

REVIEW OF THE FARMERS' QUESTION. (1870.) Paper 25

RESUMPTION! HOW IT MAY PROFITABLY BE BROUGHT
AROUT. (1869.) 8vo., paper 50

REVIEW OF THE REPORT OF HON. D. A. WELLS, Special
Commissioner of the Revenue. (1869.) 8vo., paper 50

SHALL WE HAVE PEACE? Peace Financial and Peace Political. Letters to the President Elect. (1868.) 8vo., paper 50

THE FINANCE MINISTER AND THE CURRENCY, AND
THE PUBLIC DEBT. (1868.) 8vo., paper . . 50

THE WAY TO OUTDO ENGLAND WITHOUT FIGHTING
HER. Letters to Hon. Schuyler Colfax. (1865.) 8vo., paper
$1 00

WEALTH! OF WHAT DOES IT CONSIST? (1870.) Paper 25

CAMUS.—A TREATISE ON THE TEETH OF WHEELS:
Demonstrating the best forms which can be given to them for the
purposes of Machinery, such as Mill-work and Clock-work. Translated from the French of M. Camus. By John I. Hawkins.
Illustrated by 40 plates. 8vo. $3 00

COXE.—MINING LEGISLATION.
A paper read before the Am. Social Science Association. By
Eckley B. Coxe. Paper 20

COLBURN.—THE GAS-WORKS OF LONDON:
Comprising a sketch of the Gas-works of the city, Process of
Manufacture, Quantity Produced, Cost, Profit, etc. By Zerah
Colburn. 8vo., cloth 75

COLBURN.—THE LOCOMOTIVE ENGINE:
Including a Description of its Structure, Rules for Estimat-
ing its Capabilities, and Practical Observations on its Construction and Management. By Zerah Colburn. Illustrated. A
new edition. 12mo. $1 25

COLBURN AND MAW.—THE WATER-WORKS OF LONDON:
Together with a Series of Articles on various other Water-
works. By Zerah Colburn and W. Maw. Reprinted from
"Engineering." In one volume, 8vo. . . $4 00

DAGUERREOTYPIST AND PHOTOGRAPHER'S COMPANION:
12mo., cloth $1 25

DIRCKS.—PERPETUAL MOTION:

Or Search for Self-Motive Power during the 17th, 18th, and 19th centuries. Illustrated from various authentic sources in Papers, Essays, Letters, Paragraphs, and numerous Patent Specifications, with an Introductory Essay by HENRY DIRCKS, C. E. Illustrated by numerous engravings of machines. 12mo., cloth $3 50

DIXON.—THE PRACTICAL MILLWRIGHT'S AND ENGINEER'S GUIDE:

Or Tables for Finding the Diameter and Power of Cogwheels; Diameter, Weight, and Power of Shafts; Diameter and Strength of Bolts, etc. etc. By THOMAS DIXON. 12mo., cloth. $1 50

DUNCAN.—PRACTICAL SURVEYOR'S GUIDE:

Containing the necessary information to make any person, of common capacity, a finished land surveyor without the aid of a teacher. By ANDREW DUNCAN. Illustrated. 12mo., cloth.
$1 25

DUSSAUCE.—A NEW AND COMPLETE TREATISE ON THE ARTS OF TANNING, CURRYING, AND LEATHER DRESS-ING:

Comprising all the Discoveries and Improvements made in France, Great Britain, and the United States. Edited from Notes and Documents of Messrs. Sallerou, Grouvelle, Duval, Dessables, Labarraque, Payen, René, De Fontenelle, Mala-peyre, etc. etc. By Prof. H. DUSSAUCE, Chemist. Illustrated by 212 wood engravings. 8vo. $10 00

DUSSAUCE.—A GENERAL TREATISE ON THE MANUFACTURE OF SOAP, THEORETICAL AND PRACTICAL:

Comprising the Chemistry of the Art, a Description of all the Raw Materials and their Uses. Directions for the Establishment of a Soap Factory, with the necessary Apparatus, Instructions in the Manufacture of every variety of Soap, the Assay and Determination of the Value of Alkalies, Fatty Substances, Soaps, etc. etc. By PROFESSOR H. DUSSAUCE. With an Appendix, containing Ex-tracts from the Reports of the International Jury on Soaps, as exhibited in the Paris Universal Exposition, 1867, numerous Tables, etc. etc. Illustrated by engravings. In one volume 8vo. of over 800 pages $10 00

DUSSAUCE.—PRACTICAL TREATISE ON THE FABRICATION OF MATCHES, GUN COTTON, AND FULMINATING POW-DERS.

By Professor H. DUSSAUCE. 12mo. . . . $3 00

DUSSAUCE.—A PRACTICAL GUIDE FOR THE PERFUMER:
Being a New Treatise on Perfumery the most favorable to the
Beauty without being injurious to the Health, comprising a
Description of the substances used in Perfumery, the Form-
ulæ of more than one thousand Preparations, such as Cosme-
tics, Perfumed Oils, Tooth Powders, Waters, Extracts, Tinc-
tures, Infusions, Vinaigres, Essential Oils, Pastels, Creams,
Soaps, and many new Hygienic Products not hitherto described.
Edited from Notes and Documents of Messrs. Debay, Lunel,
etc. With additions by Professor H. DUSSAUCE, Chemist. 12mo.
$3 00

DUSSAUCE.—A GENERAL TREATISE ON THE MANUFACTURE
OF VINEGAR, THEORETICAL AND PRACTICAL.
Comprising the various methods, by the slow and the quick processes, with Alcohol, Wine, Grain, Cider, and Molasses, as well
as the Fabrication of Wood Vinegar, etc. By Prof. H. DUSSAUCE.
12mo. $5 00

DUPLAIS.—A COMPLETE TREATISE ON THE DISTILLATION
AND MANUFACTURE OF ALCOHOLIC LIQUORS:
From the French of M. DUPLAIS. Translated and Edited by M.
McKENNIE, M D. Illustrated by numerous large plates and wood
engravings of the best apparatus calculated for producing the
finest products. In one vol. royal 8vo. $10 00

☞ This is a treatise of the highest scientific merit and of the
greatest practical value, surpassing in these respects, as well as
in the variety of its contents, any similar volume in the English
language.

DE GRAFF.—THE GEOMETRICAL STAIR-BUILDERS' GUIDE:
Being a Plain Practical System of Hand-Railing, embracing all
its necessary Details, and Geometrically Illustrated by 22 Steel
Engravings; together with the use of the most approved principles of Practical Geometry. By SIMON DE GRAFF, Architect.
4to. $5 00

DYER AND COLOR-MAKER'S COMPANION :
Containing upwards of two hundred Receipts for making Colors, on the most approved principles, for all the various styles
and fabrics now in existence; with the Scouring Process, and
plain Directions for Preparing, Washing-off, and Finishing the
Goods. In one vol. 12mo. $1 25

EASTON.—A PRACTICAL TREATISE ON STREET OR HORSE-POWER RAILWAYS:

Their Location, Construction, and Management; with General Plans and Rules for their Organization and Operation; together with Examinations as to their Comparative Advantages over the Omnibus System, and Inquiries as to their Value for Investment; including Copies of Municipal Ordinances relating thereto. By ALEXANDER EASTON, C. E. Illustrated by 23 plates, 8vo., cloth $2 00

FORSYTH.—BOOK OF DESIGNS FOR HEAD-STONES, MURAL, AND OTHER MONUMENTS:

Containing 78 Elaborate and Exquisite Designs. By FORSYTH.

4to., cloth $5 00

*** This volume, for the beauty and variety of its designs, has never been surpassed by any publication of the kind, and should be in the hands of every marble-worker who does fine monumental work.

FAIRBAIRN.—THE PRINCIPLES OF MECHANISM AND MACHINERY OF TRANSMISSION:

Comprising the Principles of Mechanism, Wheels, and Pulleys, Strength and Proportions of Shafts, Couplings of Shafts, and Engaging and Disengaging Gear. By WILLIAM FAIRBAIRN, Esq., C. E., LL. D., F. R. S., F. G. S., Corresponding Member of the National Institute of France, and of the Royal Academy of Turin; Chevalier of the Legion of Honor, etc. etc. Beautifully illustrated by over 150 wood-cuts. In one volume 12mo.
$2 50

FAIRBAIRN.—PRIME-MOVERS:

Comprising the Accumulation of Water-power; the Construction of Water-wheels and Turbines; the Properties of Steam; the Varieties of Steam-engines and Boilers and Wind-mills. By WILLIAM FAIRBAIRN, C. E, LL. D., F. R. S., F. G. S. Author of "Principles of Mechanism and the Machinery of Transmission." With Numerous Illustrations. In one volume. (In press.)

GILBART.—A PRACTICAL TREATISE ON BANKING:

By JAMES WILLIAM GILBART. To which is added: THE NATIONAL BANK ACT AS NOW IN FORCE. 8vo. . . $4 50

GESNER.—A PRACTICAL TREATISE ON COAL, PETROLEUM, AND OTHER DISTILLED OILS.

By ABRAHAM GESNER, M. D., F. G. S. Second edition, revised and enlarged. By GEORGE WELTDEN GESNER, Consulting Chemist and Engineer. Illustrated. 8vo. . . $3 50

GOTHIC ALBUM FOR CABINET MAKERS:

Comprising a Collection of Designs for Gothic Furniture. Illustrated by twenty-three large and beautifully engraved
plates. Oblong $3 00

GRANT.—BEET-ROOT SUGAR AND CULTIVATION OF THE
BEET:

By E. B. Grant. 12mo. $1 25

GREGORY.—MATHEMATICS FOR PRACTICAL MEN:

Adapted to the Pursuits of Surveyors, Architects, Mechanics,
and Civil Engineers. By Olinthus Gregory. 8vo., plates,
cloth $3 00

GRISWOLD.—RAILROAD ENGINEER'S POCKET COMPANION.

Comprising Rules for Calculating Deflection Distances and
Angles, Tangential Distances and Angles, and all Necessary
Tables for Engineers; also the art of Levelling from Preliminary Survey to the Construction of Railroads, intended Ex-
pressly for the Young Engineer, together with Numerous Valuable Rules and Examples. By W. Griswold. 12mo., tucks.
$1 75

GUETTIER.—METALLIC ALLOYS:

Being a Practical Guide to their Chemical and Physical Properties, their Preparation, Composition, and Uses. Translated
from the French of A. Guettier, Engineer and Director of
Founderies, author of "La Fouderie en France," etc. etc. By
A. A. Fesquet, Chemist and Engineer. In one volume, 12mo.
$3 00

HATS AND FELTING:

A Practical Treatise on their Manufacture. By a Practical
Hatter. Illustrated by Drawings of Machinery, &c., 8vo.
$1 25

HAY.—THE INTERIOR DECORATOR:

The Laws of Harmonious Coloring adapted to Interior Decora-
tions: with a Practical Treatise on House-Painting. By D.
R. Hay, House-Painter and Decorator. Illustrated by a Dia-
gram of the Primary, Secondary, and Tertiary Colors. 12mo.
$2 25

HUGHES.—AMERICAN MILLER AND MILLWRIGHT'S AS-
SISTANT:

By Wm. Carter Hughes. A new edition. In one volume,
12mo. $1 50

HUNT.—THE PRACTICE OF PHOTOGRAPHY.

By ROBERT HUNT, Vice-President of the Photographic Society, London. With numerous illustrations. 12mo., cloth .   75

HURST.—A HAND-BOOK FOR ARCHITECTURAL SURVEYORS:

Comprising Formulæ useful in Designing Builders' work, Table of Weights, of the materials used in Building, Memoranda connected with Builders' work, Mensuration, the Practice of Builders' Measurement, Contracts of Labor, Valuation of Property, Summary of the Practice in Dilapidation, etc. etc. By J. F. HURST, C. E. 2d edition, pocket-book form, full bound $2 50

JERVIS.—RAILWAY PROPERTY:

A Treatise on the Construction and Management of Railways; designed to afford useful knowledge, in the popular style, to the holders of this class of property; as well as Railway Managers, Officers, and Agents. By JOHN B. JERVIS, late Chief Engineer of the Hudson River Railroad, Croton Aqueduct, &c. One vol. 12mo., cloth   .   .   .   .   . ·$2 00

JOHNSON.—A REPORT TO THE NAVY DEPARTMENT OF THE UNITED STATES ON AMERICAN COALS:

Applicable to Steam Navigation and to other purposes. By WALTER R. JOHNSON. With numerous illustrations. 607 pp. 8vo.,   ` $10 00

JOHNSTON.—INSTRUCTIONS FOR THE ANALYSIS OF SOILS, LIMESTONES, AND MANURES.

By J. W. F. JOHNSTON. 12mo.   35

KEENE.—A HAND-BOOK OF PRACTICAL GAUGING,

For the Use of Beginners, to which is added a Chapter on Distillation, describing the process in operation at the Custom House for ascertaining the strength of wines. By JAMES B. KEENE, of H. M. Customs. 8vo.   .   .   . $1 25

KENTISH.—A TREATISE ON A BOX OF INSTRUMENTS,

And the Slide Rule; with the Theory of Trigonometry and Lo-
garithms, including Practical Geometry, Surveying, Measur-
ing of Timber, Cask and Malt Gauging, Heights, and Distances.
By THOMAS KENTISH. In one volume. 12mo. . . $1 25

KOBELL.—ERNI.—MINERALOGY SIMPLIFIED:

A short method of Determining and Classifying Minerals, by
means of simple Chemical Experiments in the Wet Way.
Translated from the last German Edition of F. VON KOBELL,
with an Introduction to Blowpipe Analysis and other additions. By HENRI ERNI, M. D., Chief Chemist, Department of
Agriculture, author of "Coal Oil and Petroleum." In one
volume. 12mo. $2 50

LANDRIN.—A TREATISE ON STEEL:

Comprising its Theory, Metallurgy, Properties, Practical Working, and Use. By M. H. C. LANDRIN, Jr., Civil Engineer.
Translated from the French, with Notes, by A. A. FESQUET,
Chemist and Engineer. With an Appendix on the Bessemer
and the Martin Processes for Manufacturing Steel, from the
Report of ABRAM S. HEWITT, United States Commissioner to
the Universal Exposition, Paris, 1867. 12mo. . . $3 00

LARKIN.—THE PRACTICAL BRASS AND IRON FOUNDER'S
GUIDE.

A Concise Treatise on Brass Founding, Moulding, the Metals
and their Alloys, etc.; to which are added Recent Improvements in the Manufacture of Iron, Steel by the Bessemer Process, etc. etc. By JAMES LARKIN, late Conductor of the Brass
Foundry Department in Reany, Neafie & Co.'s Penn Works,
Philadelphia. Fifth edition, revised, with extensive Additions. In one volume. 12mo. $2 25

LEAVITT.—FACTS ABOUT PEAT AS AN ARTICLE OF FUEL:
With Remarks upon its Origin and Composition, the Localities in which it is found, the Methods of Preparation and Manufacture, and the various Uses to which it is applicable; together with many other matters of Practical and Scientific Interest. To which is added a chapter on the Utilization of Coal Dust with Peat for the Production of an Excellent Fuel at Moderate Cost, especially adapted for Steam Service. By H. T. Leavitt. Third edition. 12mo.   .   .   . $1 75

LEROUX.—A PRACTICAL TREATISE ON THE MANUFAC-TURE OF WORSTEDS AND CARDED YARNS:
Translated from the French of Charles Leroux, Mechanical Engineer, and Superintendent of a Spinning Mill. By Dr H. Paine, and A. A. Fesquet. Illustrated by 12 large plates. In one volume 8vo. $5 00

LESLIE (MISS).—COMPLETE COOKERY:
Directions for Cookery in its Various Branches. By Miss Leslie. 60th edition. Thoroughly revised, with the addition of New Receipts. In 1 vol. 12mo., cloth   .   . $1 50

LESLIE (MISS). LADIES' HOUSE BOOK:
a Manual of Domestic Economy. 20th revised edition. 12mo., cloth $1 25

LESLIE (MISS).—TWO HUNDRED RECEIPTS IN FRENCH COOKERY.
12mo.   50

LIEBER.—ASSAYER'S GUIDE:
Or, Practical Directions to Assayers, Miners, and Smelters, for the Tests and Assays, by Heat and by Wet Processes, for the Ores of all the principal Metals, of Gold and Silver Coins and Alloys, and of Coal, etc. By Oscar M. Lieber. 12mo., cloth $1 25

LOVE.—THE ART OF DYEING, CLEANING, SCOURING, AND FINISHING:
On the most approved English and French methods; being Practical Instructions in Dyeing Silks, Woollens, and Cottons, Feathers, Chips, Straw, etc.; Scouring and Cleaning Bed and Window Curtains, Carpets, Rugs, etc.; French and English Cleaning, etc. By Thomas Love. Second American Edition, to which are added General Instructions for the Use of Aniline Colors. 8vo. 5 00

MAIN AND BROWN.—QUESTIONS ON SUBJECTS CONNECTED WITH THE MARINE STEAM-ENGINE:

And Examination Papers; with Hints for their Solution. By THOMAS J. MAIN, Professor of Mathematics, Royal Naval College, and THOMAS BROWN, Chief Engineer, R. N. 12mo., cloth $1 50

MAIN AND BROWN.—THE INDICATOR AND DYNAMOMETER:

With their Practical Applications to the Steam-Engine. By THOMAS J. MAIN, M. A. F. R., Ass't Prof. Royal Naval College, Portsmouth, and THOMAS BROWN, Assoc. Inst. C. E., Chief Engineer, R. N., attached to the R. N. College. Illustrated. From the Fourth London Edition. 8vo. . . . `. $1 50

MAIN AND BROWN.—THE MARINE STEAM-ENGINE.

By THOMAS J. MAIN, F. R. Ass't S. Mathematical Professor at Royal Naval College, and THOMAS BROWN, Assoc. Inst. C. E. Chief Engineer, R. N. Attached to the Royal Naval College. Authors of "Questions Connected with the Marine Steam-Engine," and the "Indicator and Dynamometer." With numerous Illustrations. In one volume 8vo. $5 00

MARTIN.—SCREW-CUTTING TABLES, FOR THE USE OF MECHANICAL ENGINEERS:

Showing the Proper Arrangement of Wheels for Cutting the Threads of Screws of any required Pitch; with a Table for Making the Universal Gas-Pipe Thread and Taps. By W. A. MARTIN, Engineer. 8vo. 50

MILES—A PLAIN TREATISE ON HORSE-SHOEING.

With Illustrations. By WILLIAM MILES, author of "The Horse's Foot"

MOLESWORTH.—POCKET-BOOK OF USEFUL FORMULÆ AND MEMORANDA FOR CIVIL AND MECHANICAL ENGINEERS.

By GUILFORD L. MOLESWORTH, Member of the Institution of Civil Engineers, Chief Resident Engineer of the Ceylon Railway. Second American from the Tenth London Edition. In one volume, full bound in pocket-book form $2 00

MOORE.—THE INVENTOR'S GUIDE:

Patent Office and Patent Laws: or, a Guide to Inventors, and a Book of Reference for Judges, Lawyers, Magistrates, and others. By J G. MOORE. 12mo., cloth $1 25

NAPIER.—A MANUAL OF ELECTRO-METALLURGY:

Including the Application of the Art to Manufacturing Processes. By JAMES NAPIER. Fourth American, from the Fourth London edition, revised and enlarged. Illustrated by engravings. In one volume, 8vo. $2 00

NAPIER.—A SYSTEM OF CHEMISTRY APPLIED TO DYEING:
By JAMES NAPIER, F. C. S. A New and Thoroughly Revised Edition, completely brought up to the present state of the Science, including the Chemistry of Coal Tar Colors. By A. A. FESQUET, Chemist and Engineer. With an Appendix on Dyeing and Calico Printing, as shown at the Paris Universal Exposition of 1867, from the Reports of the International Jury, etc. Illustrated. In one volume 8vo., 400 pages $5 00

NEWBERY.—GLEANINGS FROM ORNAMENTAL ART OF EVERY STYLE;
Drawn from Examples in the British, South Kensington, Indian, Crystal Palace, and other Museums, the Exhibitions of 1851 and 1862, and the best English and Foreign works. In a series of one hundred exquisitely drawn Plates, containing many hundred examples. By ROBERT NEWBERY. 4to. $15 00

NICHOLSON.—A MANUAL OF THE ART OF BOOK-BINDING:
Containing full instructions in the different Branches of Forwarding, Gilding, and Finishing. Also, the Art of Marbling Bookedges and Paper. By JAMES B. NICHOLSON. Illustrated. 12mo. cloth $2 25

NORRIS.—A HAND-BOOK FOR LOCOMOTIVE ENGINEERS AND MACHINISTS:
Comprising the Proportions and Calculations for Constructing Locomotives; Manner of Setting Valves; Tables of Squares, Cubes, Areas, etc. etc. By SEPTIMUS NORRIS, Civil and Mechanical Engineer. New edition. Illustrated, 12mo., cloth
. $2 00

NYSTROM. — ON TECHNOLOGICAL EDUCATION AND THE CONSTRUCTION OF SHIPS AND SCREW PROPELLERS:
For Naval and Marine Engineers. By JOHN W. NYSTROM, late Acting Chief Engineer U. S. N. Second edition, revised with additional matter. Illustrated by seven engravings. 12mo.
$2 50

O'NEILL.—A DICTIONARY OF DYEING AND CALICO PRINTING:
Containing a brief account of all the Substances and Processes in use in the Art of Dyeing and Printing Textile Fabrics: with Practical Receipts and Scientific Information. By CHARLES O'NEILL, Analytical Chemist; Fellow of the Chemical Society of London; Member of the Literary and Philosophical Society of Manchester; Author of "Chemistry of Calico Printing and Dyeing." To which is added An Essay on Coal Tar Colors and their Application to

Dyeing and Calico Printing. By A. A. FESQUET, Chemist and Engineer. With an Appendix on Dyeing and Calico Printing, as shown at the Exposition of 1867, from the Reports of the Interna. tional Jury, etc. In one volume 8vo., 491 pages . . $6 00

OSBORN.—THE METALLURGY OF IRON AND STEEL:
Theoretical and Practical : In all its Branches ; With Special Reference to American Materials and Processes. By H. S. OSBORN, LL. D., Professor of Mining and Metallurgy in Lafayette College, Easton, Pa. Illustrated by 230 Engravings on Wood, and 6 Folding Plates. 8vo., 972 pages $10 00

OSBORN.—AMERICAN MINES AND MINING :
Theoretically and Practically Considered. By Prof. H. S. OS-BORN, Illustrated by numerous engravings. 8vo. (*In preparation.*)

PAINTER, GILDER, AND VARNISHER'S COMPANION :
Containing Rules and Regulations in everything relating to the Arts of Painting, Gilding, Varnishing, and Glass Staining, with numerous useful and valuable Receipts ; Tests for the Detection of Adulterations in Oils and Colors, and a statement of the Diseases and Accidents to which Painters, Gilders, and Varnishers are particularly liable, with the simplest methods of Prevention and Remedy. With Directions for Graining, Marbling, Sign Writing, and Gilding on Glass. To which are added COMPLETE INSTRUCTIONS FOR COACH PAINTING AND VARNISHING. 12mo., cloth, $1 50

PALLETT. —THE MILLER'S, MILLWRIGHT'S, AND ENGINEER'S GUIDE.
By HENRY PALLETT. Illustrated. In one vol. 12mo. . $3 00

PERKINS.—GAS AND VENTILATION.
Practical Treatise on Gas and Ventilation. With Special Relation to Illuminating, Heating, and Cooking by Gas. Including Scientific Helps to Engineer-students and others. With illustrated Diagrams. By E. E. PERKINS. 12mo., cloth . . . $1 25

PERKINS AND STOWE.—A NEW GUIDE TO THE SHEET-IRON AND BOILER PLATE ROLLER :
Containing a Series of Tables showing the Weight of Slabs and Piles to Produce Boiler Plates, and of the Weight of Piles and the Sizes of Bars to Produce Sheet-iron ; the Thickness of the Bar Gauge in Decimals ; the Weight per foot, and the Thickness on the Bar or Wire Gauge of the fractional parts of an inch ; the Weight per sheet, and the Thickness on the Wire Gauge of Sheet-Iron of various dimensions to weigh 112 lbs. per bundle ; and the conversion of Short Weight into Long Weight, and Long Weight into Short. Estimated and collected by G. H. PERKINS and J. G· STOWE $2 50

PHILLIPS AND DARLINGTON.—RECORDS OF MINING AND METALLURGY:

Or, Facts and Memoranda for the use of the Mine Agent and Smelter. By J. ARTHUR PHILLIPS, Mining Engineer, Graduate of the Imperial School of Mines, France, etc., and JOHN DARLINGTON. Illustrated by numerous engravings. In one vol. 12mo. . $2 00

PRADAL, MALEPEYRE, AND DUSSAUCE.—A COMPLETE TREATISE ON PERFUMERY:

Containing notices of the Raw Material used in the Art, and the Best Formulæ. According to the most approved Methods followed in France, England, and the United States. By M. P. PRADAL, Perfumer-Chemist, and M. F. MALEPEYRE. Translated from the French, with extensive additions, by Prof. H. DUSSAUCE. 8vo. $10

PROTEAUX.—PRACTICAL GUIDE FOR THE MANUFACTURE OF PAPER AND BOARDS.

By A. PROTEAUX, Civil Engineer, and Graduate of the School of Arts and Manufactures, Director of Thiers's Paper Mill, 'Puy-de-Dôme. With additions, by L. S. LE NORMAND. Translated from the French, with Notes, by HORATIO PAINE, A. B., M. D. To which is added a Chapter on the Manufacture of Paper from Wood in the United States, by HENRY T. BROWN, of the "American Artisan." Illustrated by six plates, containing Drawings of Raw Materials, Machinery, Plans of Paper-Mills, etc. etc. 8vo. $5 00

REGNAULT.—ELEMENTS OF CHEMISTRY.

By M. V. REGNAULT. Translated from the French by T. FORREST BENTON, M. B., and edited, with notes, by JAMES C. BOOTH, Melter and Refiner U. S. Mint, and WM. L. FABER, Metallurgist and Mining Engineer. Illustrated by nearly 700 wood engravings. Comprising nearly 1500 pages. In two vols. 8vo., cloth $10 00

REID.—A PRACTICAL TREATISE ON THE MANUFACTURE OF PORTLAND CEMENT:

By HENRY REID, C. E. To which is added a Translation of M. A. Lipowitz's Work, describing a new method adopted in Germany of Manufacturing that Cement. By W. F. REID. Illustrated by plates and wood engravings. 8vo. $7 00

RIFFAULT, VERGNAUD, AND TOUSSAINT.—A PRACTICAL TREATISE ON THE MANUFACTURE OF COLORS FOR PAINTING:

Containing the best Formulæ and the Processes the Newest and in most General Use. By MM. RIFFAULT, VERGNAUD, and TOUSSAINT. Revised and Edited by M. F. MALEPEYRE and Dr. EMIL WINCKLER. Illustrated by Engravings. In one vol. 8vo. (*In preparation.*)

RIFFAULT, VERGNAUD, AND TOUSSAINT.—A PRACTICAL TREATISE ON THE MANUFACTURE OF VARNISHES:
By MM. RIFFAULT, VERGNAUD, and TOUSSAINT. Revised and Edited by M. F. MALEPEYRE and Dr. EMIL WINCKLER. Illustrated. In one vol. 8vo. (*In preparation.*)

SHUNK.—A PRACTICAL TREATISE ON RAILWAY CURVES AND LOCATION, FOR YOUNG ENGINEERS.
By WM. F. SHUNK, Civil Engineer. 12mo., tucks . . $2 00

SMEATON.—BUILDER'S POCKET COMPANION:
Containing the Elements of Building, Surveying, and Architecture ; with Practical Rules and Instructions connected with the subject. By A. C. SMEATON, Civil Engineer, etc. In one volume, 12mo. $1 50

SMITH.—THE DYER'S INSTRUCTOR:
Comprising Practical Instructions in the Art of Dyeing Silk, Cotton, Wool, and Worsted, and Woollen Goods : containing nearly 800 Receipts. To which is added a Treatise on the Art of Padding ; and the Printing of Silk Warps, Skeins, and Handkerchiefs, and the various Mordants and Colors for the different styles of such work. By DAVID SMITH, Pattern Dyer, 12mo., cloth
$3 00

SMITH.—THE PRACTICAL DYER'S GUIDE:
Comprising Practical Instructions in the Dyeing of Shot Cobourgs, Silk Striped Orleans, Colored Orleans from Black Warps, ditto from White Warps, Colored Cobourgs from White Warps, Merinos, Yarns, Woollen Cloths, etc. Containing nearly 300 Receipts, to most of which a Dyed Pattern is annexed. Also, a Treatise on the Art of Padding. By DAVID SMITH. In one vol. 8vo. $25 00

SHAW.—CIVIL ARCHITECTURE:
Being a Complete Theoretical and Practical System of Building, containing the Fundamental Principles of the Art. By EDWARD SHAW, Architect. To which is added a Treatise on Gothic Architecture, &c. By THOMAS W. SILLOWAY and GEORGE M. HARDING, Architects. The whole illustrated by 102 quarto plates finely engraved on copper. Eleventh Edition. 4to. Cloth. $10 00

SLOAN.—AMERICAN HOUSES:
A variety of Original Designs for Rural Buildings. Illustrated by 26 colored Engravings, with Descriptive References. By SAMUEL SLOAN, Architect, author of the "Model Architect," etc. etc. 8vo.
$2 50

SCHINZ.—RESEARCHES ON THE ACTION OF THE BLAST FURNACE.
By CHAS. SCHINZ. Seven plates. 12mo. . . . $4 25

SMITH.—PARKS AND PLEASURE GROUNDS:

Or, Practical Notes on Country Residences, Villas, Public Parks, and Gardens. By CHARLES H. J. SMITH, Landscape Gardener and Garden Architect, etc. etc. 12mo. $2 25

STOKES.—CABINET-MAKER'S AND UPHOLSTERER'S COMPANION:

Comprising the Rudiments and Principles of Cabinet-making and Upholstery, with Familiar Instructions, Illustrated by Examples for attaining a Proficiency in the Art of Drawing, as applicable to Cabinet-work; The Processes of Veneering, Inlaying, and Buhl-work; the Art of Dyeing and Staining Wood, Bone, Tortoise Shell, etc. Directions for Lackering, Japanning, and Varnishing; to make French Polish; to prepare the Best Glues, Cements, and Compositions, and a number of Receipts, particularly for workmen generally. By J. STOKES. In one vol. 12mo. With illustrations
$1 25

STRENGTH AND OTHER PROPERTIES OF METALS.

Reports of Experiments on the Strength and other Properties of Metals for Cannon. With a Description of the Machines for Testing Metals, and of the Classification of Cannon in service. By Officers of the Ordnance Department U. S. Army. By authority of the Secretary of War. Illustrated by 25 large steel plates. In 1 vol. quarto $10 00

SULLIVAN.—PROTECTION TO NATIVE INDUSTRY.

By Sir EDWARD SULLIVAN, Baronet. (1870.) 8vo. . $1 50

TABLES SHOWING THE WEIGHT OF ROUND, SQUARE, AND FLAT BAR IRON, STEEL, ETC.

By Measurement. Cloth 63

TAYLOR.—STATISTICS OF COAL:

Including Mineral Bituminous Substances employed in Arts and Manufactures; with their Geographical, Geological, and Commercial Distribution and amount of Production and Consumption on the American Continent. With Incidental Statistics of the Iron Manufacture. By R. C. TAYLOR. Second edition, revised by S. S. HALDEMAN. Illustrated by five Maps and many wood engravings. 8vo., cloth $6 00

TEMPLETON.—THE PRACTICAL EXAMINATOR ON STEAM AND THE STEAM-ENGINE:

With Instructive References relative thereto, for the Use of Engineers, Students, and others. By WM. TEMPLETON, Engineer. 12mo.
$1 25

THOMAS.—THE MODERN PRACTICE OF PHOTOGRAPHY.
By R. W. THOMAS, F. C. S. 8vo., cloth 75

THOMSON.—FREIGHT CHARGES CALCULATOR.
By ANDREW THOMSON, Freight Agent $1 25

TURNING: SPECIMENS OF FANCY TURNING EXECUTED ON THE HAND OR FOOT LATHE:
With Geometric, Oval, and Eccentric Chucks, and Elliptical Cutting Frame. By an Amateur. Illustrated by 30 exquisite Photographs. 4to. $3 00

TURNER'S (THE) COMPANION:
Containing Instructions in Concentric, Elliptic, and Eccentric Turning; also various Plates of Chucks, Tools, and Instruments; and Directions for using the Eccentric Cutter, Drill, Vertical Cutter, and Circular Rest; with Patterns and Instructions for working them. A new edition in 1 vol. 12mo. $1 50

URBIN—BRULL.—A PRACTICAL GUIDE FOR PUDDLING IRON AND STEEL.
By ED. URBIN, Engineer of Arts and Manufactures. A Prize Essay read before the Association of Engineers, Graduate of the School of Mines, of Liege, Belgium, at the Meeting of 1865-6. To which is added a COMPARISON OF THE RESISTING PROPERTIES OF IRON AND STEEL. By A. BRULL. Translated from the French by A. A. FESQUET, Chemist and Engineer. In one volume, 8vo.
$1 00

VOGDES.—THE ARCHITECT'S AND BUILDER'S POCKET COMPANION AND PRICE BOOK.
By F. W. VOGDES, Architect. Illustrated. Full bound in pocketbook form. $2 00
In book form, 18mo., muslin 1 50

WARN.—THE SHEET METAL WORKER'S INSTRUCTOR, FOR ZINC, SHEET-IRON, COPPER AND TIN PLATE WORKERS, &c.
By REUBEN HENRY WARN, Practical Tin Plate Worker. Illustrated by 32 plates and 37 wood engravings. 8vo. . . $3 00

WATSON.—A MANUAL OF THE HAND-LATHE.
By EGBERT P. WATSON, Late of the "Scientific American," Author of "Modern Practice of American Machinists and Engineers," In one volume, 12mo. $1 50

WATSON.—THE MODERN PRACTICE OF AMERICAN MA-
CHINISTS AND ENGINEERS:

Including the Construction, Application, and Use of Drills, Lathe
Tools, Cutters for Boring Cylinders, and Hollow Work Generally,
with the most Economical Speed of the same, the Results verified
by Actual Practice at the Lathe, the Vice, and on the Floor.
Together with Workshop management, Economy of Manufacture,
the Steam-Engine, Boilers, Gears, Belting, etc. etc. By EGBERT
P. WATSON, late of the "Scientific American." Illustrated by
eighty-six engravings. 12mo. $2 50

WATSON.—THE THEORY AND PRACTICE OF THE ART OF
WEAVING BY HAND AND POWER:

With Calculations and Tables for the use of those connected with
the Trade. By JOHN WATSON, Manufacturer and Practical Machine
Maker. Illustrated by large drawings of the best Power-Looms.
8vo. $10 00

WEATHERLY.—TREATISE ON THE ART OF BOILING SU-
GAR, CRYSTALLIZING, LOZENGE-MAKING, COMFITS,
GUM GOODS,

And other processes for Confectionery, &c. In which are explained, in an easy and familiar manner, the various Methods
of Manufacturing every description of Raw and Refined Sugar
Goods, as sold by Confectioners and others   .   .   . $2 00

WILL.—TABLES FOR QUALITATIVE CHEMICAL ANALYSIS.
By Prof. HEINRICH WILL, of Giessen, Germany. Seventh edi-
tion. Translated by CHARLES F. HIMES, Ph. D., Professor of
Natural Science, Dickinson College, Carlisle, Pa.   .   . $1 25

WILLIAMS.—ON HEAT AND STEAM:
Embracing New Views of Vaporization, Condensation, and Expansion. By CHARLES WYE WILLIAMS, A. I. C. E. Illustrated. 8vo.
$3 50

WORSSAM.—ON MECHANICAL SAWS:
From the Transactions of the Society of Engineers, 1867. By
S. W. WORSSAM, Jr. Illustrated by 18 large folding plates. 8vo.
$5 00

WÖHLER.—A HAND-BOOK OF MINERAL ANALYSIS.
By F. WÖHLER. Edited by H. B. NASON, Professor of Chemistry,
Rensselaer Institute, Troy, N. Y. With numerous Illustrations.
12mo. $3 00

LaVergne, TN USA
04 May 2010
181490LV00003B/62/P

9 781147 488173